# Motivational English for At-Risk Students

## A Language Arts Course That Works

Marge Christensen

National Educational Service
Bloomington, Indiana    1992

Cover Design by Bryan Thatcher

recycled paper

Printed in the United States of America
ISBN 1-879639-19-X

# Dedication

This book is dedicated to my students, especially Paul, Andy, Dawn, Africa, Denisha, Maria, Juan, Alvaro, and Jimmy, who have taught me an infinite amount about the learning process, and about the joys of teaching.

# About the Author

Marge Christensen is a high school English teacher, who has worked for five years as the teacher/coordinator of a special program for at-risk high school students in Tucson, Arizona. The program, which has been highly successful, is a computerized language arts class, funded in partnership between the Arizona Supreme Court and the Tucson Unified School District. Christensen started with the original program, PALS (Principle of the Alphabet Literacy System), a 20-week IBM program, and expanded it into a comprehensive 3-year English course geared to make at-risk students experience success and build self-esteem, in addition to improve reading, writing, and thinking skills. Fourteen other labs in the Arizona Supreme Court network have now instituted her program. Christensen holds a Bachelor of Arts in English and a Master of Arts in Administration and Supervision in Education.

Her graduate research project examined the expanded PALS program and its impact on four target populations. She has made numerous presentations for educators, and has been a speaker at state and national literacy conferences.

# Table of Contents

# Preface

The language arts course presented in this volume evolved from four years of work with at-risk students at an inner city high school in Tucson, Arizona, with a largely multicultural population. As teacher/coordinator of a special English program for at-risk students, I was able to expand the original 20-week IBM computerized literacy program called PALS (Principle of the Alphabet Literacy System) into a 3-year program specially designed to effectively meet the needs of this population and to enable them to experience a high degree of success.

Students in this program have measurably improved in reading and writing skills. Equally as significant, however, is the dramatic improvement they have demonstrated in the areas of self-esteem and self-confidence. An example of this is that of the twenty students in the program who earned their high school diplomas in 1991, eighteen plan to go on to further their education at the community college level. One student entered the U.S. Air Force.

The program has received a great deal of acclaim both within Arizona and from other states. It is being replicated already in fourteen other Arizona school districts. In the language arts course outlined in this volume, it is the intent of the author to share those elements which have contributed to the success of this program with other teachers of at-risk students.

I have identified those elements which I believe are responsible for the success of the program and have incorporated them into a one-year motivational language arts course for at-risk high school students.

The book is intended as a practical, easily implemented tool for teachers and program administrators. It begins with a discussion of the **innovative learning environment**, which, in this case, is set up as a professional office setting. It further explains how to make the learning environment responsive to at-risk students' need to belong, and how to develop self-esteem and personal and social responsibility. The roles of the **student as office worker** and of the **teacher as manager** and support group member are also covered.

**Self-esteem** is a crucial requisite for learning and for personal success. Therefore, an entire chapter is devoted to how to promote self-esteem among students. This includes a description of **specific motivational strategies**, involvement of **peer educators**, and an **extended school family or support group for students**, as well as grading policy.

Research indicates that cooperative learning strategies are highly effective in developing improved self-esteem and a sense of shared responsibility and positive interdependence with others. A chapter devoted to **cooperative learning** explains this teaching strategy in depth. Numerous cooperative learning activities for language arts lessons are included throughout the book.

The remaining chapters are devoted primarily to the actual content of the course, and cover such areas as the writing process, reading comprehension, a whole language approach to literature, vocabulary development, career exploration, goal setting, and job skills.

Also, a chapter on **parent involvement** is included since the family is the most crucial social unit in a child's life and development. The parents' self-esteem is crucial to their ability to nurture their children's positive self-esteem and personal responsibility. In many cases, parents need help in developing their own self-esteem.

The final chapter is devoted to **public relations**, because it is vital to the success of the program itself as well as to public education in general in this country, that every teacher today become an effective public relations agent. The prevailing attitude toward education in the U.S. today is that schools can repair all of society's ills and that they can accomplish this with radically decreased funding and even fewer resources. In the U.S., the vast majority of taxpayers do not have children in school. Therefore, educators have been thrust into the role of constantly having to promote education to the voters and having to work diligently to reverse the negative image that the voters have of education and educators. Furthermore, it is extremely beneficial to our schools and to our students to involve business and community resources in the educational process, and to establish partnerships between schools and these sectors. There are many ways in which teachers can have a powerful impact in building linkages between school, business, community, and parents. The need for such partnerships is becoming increasingly more urgent as the population of students at-risk of dropping out continues to increase dramatically.

It is critical that schools be sensitive and responsive to the needs of students who are at-risk of becoming school dropouts. National statistics indicate that each year almost a million students dropout of school largely to escape failure. The price tag for this national tragedy is too costly for our society to pay. Statistics indicate that only two years after they leave school, dropouts are

- More than 3 times as likely as graduates to be unemployed.
- More than 4 times as likely as graduates to become involved in crime.
- If female (married or not), 6 times as likely as graduates to give birth.
- If female, more than 9 times as likely as graduates to be on welfare.

In comparison to the cost to the community for the dropout problem, the cost of implementing special courses which are geared to respond to the needs of at-risk students is a social and economic bargain.

If the American public is serious and sincere about wanting to rectify the shortcomings of our nation's failing educational system, then that commitment must include the implementation of courses such as this one for students who are potential dropouts.

# 1

# The Learning Environment

## THE CLASSROOM

IN PREPARING THE CLASSROOM for this course, it is of utmost importance to create an innovative learning environment which will be a positive, comfortable place for students, and one which they can "buy into" and in which they will take ownership. It needs to be "their place," and it needs to be a special place.

Keep in mind that for this population of students, school has been a negative and sometimes painful place. Typically they associate school with failure. The classroom is a constant reminder for them of their past lack of success. Therefore, the first step in preparing the classroom for this class is to remove any semblance of a typical classroom from the room. That includes eliminating the school desks, chalkboards, and even the school clock.

The learning environment for this particular course is intended to be that of a professional office environment. This requires painting the room (off-white color recommended), with perhaps a graphic art design on one wall. The floor should be carpeted, and plants and artwork should be used to decorate the room.

This may sound costly. However, it need not be. I was able to accomplish all of this for just under $175, which was the cost of paint for the walls and for the graphic art design as well as brushes and rollers. Volunteers painted the room, and an interior design company donated the carpeting. Silk plants and art work for the walls were also donated. It may take some work to accomplish this, but it is worth the effort to create an environment conducive to motivating at-risk students and to building their self-esteem. The professional office setting contributes to achieving both of these ends.

Once the room is prepared, it is necessary to obtain tables or desks and fifteen office swivel chairs for the students. If at all possible, avoid using classroom chairs with arms with writing surfaces. These åre not only uncomfortable, they are also typical classroom furniture. It is important to make the room unlike a classroom and more like an office setting.

## THE EQUIPMENT

The course is designed to utilize five IBM or IBM compatible computers with color monitors and one printer. The computers should have at least 640K of memory. Ideally, the room should be equipped with fifteen computers, or one per student. However, the financial constraints imposed upon most school districts may make this an unattainable goal.

Computers not only give the students high tech skills, but also contribute to giving them self-confidence and self-esteem. Computers allow students to progress at their own pace and are non-threatening to students. Moreover, they make it possible for the teacher to circulate throughout the room and give more one on one attention and personal support to the students.

The room arrangement and particularly the positioning of the computers will be determined largely by the location of electrical outlets. However, if possible, avoid placing the computers in a straight row and thereby presenting an image of the typical classroom computer lab. Try to arrange the tables and chairs into five independent work areas (or departments) for three students each, and include one computer at each work station. In the center of the room, place one or two round tables with chairs. These are to be used for writing or small group meetings.

Another necessary item in this classroom is a telephone. This allows the teacher to call for computer repairs, as well as to contact numerous community resources for the students. These resources could include guest speakers, businesses for opportunities in career shadowing, community college, sources of information on college scholarships, probation officers, and social services. The telephone is another visual reminder that this classroom is different. It is a professional office setting. The telephone also is the tool that puts numerous resources for students at the teacher's fingertips.

## STUDENTS' ROLE IN THIS CLASSROOM

Students in this class function as office workers. They behave professionally, use office skills, take pride in their workplace, and keep their workstations clean. They take proper care of the equipment; they pass in their work on time (except when they are engaged in self-paced work). They do not line up at the door at quitting time; they are cooperative and treat co-workers with respect. They become independent, self-directed learners who take responsibility for their own work and progress. They assume this role because they are treated as adult, professional office workers, and because they are able to see a relevancy between the work they do in this class and the work they will perform in the actual employment workplace.

Upon entering the class, students should be required to sign a contract stating their agreement to take proper care of the equipment, to refrain from preventing others from learning, and to avoid absenteeism. Any student violating the contract should be removed from the course for the remainder of the year. Students generally like this class, and they do not want to jeopardize their chances of remaining in the program, so very few of them violate their contracts.

## THE ROLE OF THE TEACHER IN THIS COURSE

In this course, the teacher's role is manager and support person for the students. In a way, the teacher is a sort of extended school family for the student. The teacher is still the provider of the instruction, but the position entails a great deal more than simply presenting the instruction. The teacher must try to do everything possible to ensure that the students experience success in school. This includes talking to the students individually and giving them generous doses of encouragement. The teacher's role as support person for the students will be discussed in greater depth in the chapter on self-esteem.

## CLASS SIZE

In order to be able to adequately implement the program described above, it is imperative that the maximum class size in this class be fifteen. Increasing this maximum class size by any significant number of students would eliminate any possibility of one on one attention for these students and would defeat the purpose of the course, which is to motivate at-risk students to succeed in school.

# 2

# Self-Esteem

IN JANUARY, 1990, the California State Department of Education published a report of the California Task Force to Promote Self-Esteem and Personal and Social Responsibility, which defined self-esteem as: *"Appreciating my own worth and importance and having the character to be accountable for myself and to act responsibly toward others."*

A key finding of the Task Force was that *self-esteem* is the best candidate for a *"social vaccine* — something that empowers us to live responsibly and that inoculates us against the lures of crime, violence, substance abuse, teen pregnancy, child abuse, chronic welfare dependency, and educational failure."

The Task Force also found that the school environment plays a major role in a student's development of self-esteem. Also, young women who have self-esteem are less likely to become pregnant as teenagers. People who have self-esteem are less likely to engage in destructive or self-destructive behavior, including child abuse, substance abuse, crime or violence. One crucial factor for nurturing self-esteem is an affirming school environment.

Some of the recommendations of the Task Force aimed specifically at education and at preventing academic failure are:

1. Self-esteem and responsibility must be incorporated into the total education program.

2. A real-life skills curriculum should be instituted.

3. Schools need to promote more parent involvement.

4. Educators and schools must be sensitive to the needs of students at-risk of failure.

5. Peer counseling for students should be instituted.

6. Schools should provide cooperative learning opportunities.

7. Class size or student-adult ratios must be reduced.

These recommendations from the California Task Force to Promote Self-Esteem were very welcome news to me, as I have been implementing them into the program for at-risk students I have coordinated for the past four years. I have observed first-hand the effectiveness of these recommendations.

The following present specific, detailed ideas and methods for implementing these recommendations into the language arts program for at-risk students:

## INCORPORATING SELF-ESTEEM AND RESPONSIBILITY INTO THE PROGRAM

### Office Worker of the Week

It is important to recognize students' successes, even the small successes. In keeping with the office environment of the classroom and the emphasis on professional office behavior, one way to recognize students and to build self-esteem is to present a weekly *Office Worker of the Week Award*. Since students are not employees, an Employee of the Week Award is impossible, but the Office Worker Award is a good substitute. Simply tell the students that each week one student will be recognized for excellent work and for a good attitude. Print that student's name and post it on a bulletin board with a label, "Office Worker of the Week." Present that student with some small gift or award and make the presentation a big event. Try to recognize as many students as possible during the year. Since the award is simply for being the best worker of that particular week, it may be used to recognize the student who did a good job for the first time that particular week as well as to recognize those students who do well most of the time.

### Contests

At-risk students need large doses of positive feedback. One way to give them recognition and make them feel pride in their work and accomplishments is to have contests and to recognize the winners for their achievements. Contests may be held for the best essay or for the best letter to President of the U.S. (if you have them write such a letter) or for the best business letter and job application for hypothetical jobs.

Contests are also a vehicle for rewarding for non-academic achievements, such as for being the most helpful to other students or for the best attendance. The important point is to allow them to experience success as much as possible.

### Student Acceptance of Responsibility

It is vitally important to get students to buy-in to the program and to feel that this is *their* workplace and that it is a really exciting place. I have experienced a high degree of success in this area by simply making students responsible for the care of the lab. This includes daily vacuuming of the carpet; cleaning the computers and tables two or three times a week; keeping their disks, folders, books, and papers all in their proper places; and keeping their workplaces clean and orderly. Emphasize the idea that professional office workers take care of their work areas, and that it is not professional in the job world to do such things as line up at the door at quitting time, leave paper in the desk, or leave materials lying around. Students really respond positively to this type of atmosphere, and begin to develop pride in their workplace and in themselves.

Also require students to take responsibility for entering the room, getting their disks and materials, and going to their work stations and getting to work. Again, stress that professional office workers do not sit idle, waiting for the boss to take them by the hand and tell them what to do. However, by the same token, ensure that students are given clear, specific instructions as to the work they are to do and what to progress to when they complete their work.

### Allow the Students to "Shine" in Their Workplace

When possible, hold open houses and invite dignitaries, parents, or school officials and give the students an opportunity to show their knowledge of the programs and to demonstrate the equipment. Let *the students* do the tours and the talking, and display their essays on the bulletin board. Give the students as many opportunities as possible to "shine" and to feel important. Even having guests visit the classroom offers great opportunities for the more proficient students to take the visitor on a tour of the workplace and to explain the program. This makes them feel important and helps to develop pride in their work and their program.

Take photographs during these events and display them in frames in the lab. Students love to see their pictures hanging on the wall. Keep a Guest Book and have students ask guests to sign it so that you can keep a record of guests who visit the classroom.

## Publication of Student Writing

Whenever possible, try to publish students' writing in periodicals or student publications. Another possibility is to use your computers and a desktop publishing program to publish your own literary magazine.

Seeing their names and writing in print makes students feel important and helps to build self-esteem.

## INSTITUTING A REAL-LIFE SKILLS CURRICULUM

At-risk students often do not attend school regularly because they are not able to see any relevance between what is taught in school and issues and situations they face in the real world. The language arts course presented here has incorporated into it real life skills in order to address this need. For instance, it includes a unit on job skills and career research and exploration. In addition, the professional office environment promotes the teaching of behavioral skills for the workplace. Moreover, some of the software on reading comprehension includes such skills as using a checkbook, reading graphs and charts, distinguishing between fact and opinion, understanding arguments, using critical thinking skills. Furthermore, the chapter on Reading Comprehension includes an extremely effective 3-tiered program, called *Reading Realities*, which is designed specifically for at-risk students. This program includes Real Life Issues, which deals with actual issues facing teenagers, such as addiction, alcoholism, teen pregnancy, shoplifting, dropping out. All of these components of this course focus on real-life skills which have some relevance to the real world of the at-risk student.

## PROMOTING PARENTAL INVOLVEMENT

In order for parents to provide an environment that promotes and nurtures the development of self-esteem for their youngsters, the parents must themselves have high self-esteem. A very large percentage of at-risk students are reading well below their grade level. In fact, many of them are functionally illiterate; i.e., they are reading at or below the 5th grade level. Add to this the fact that many children who are functionally illiterate also have parents who are functionally or entirely illiterate. This situation creates the sad likelihood that most at-risk students will not come from home environments where the development of self-esteem is fostered.

Therefore, schools need to assist parents of our at-risk students in developing their own self-esteem in order to help them to become more capable and successful at nurturing their children's self-esteem and personal responsibility.

A later chapter in this book is devoted to encouraging parental involvement and to establishing an evening literacy class for parents.

## BE SENSITIVE TO NEEDS OF STUDENTS AT-RISK OF FAILURE

The role of the teacher as support person and extended family, and the addition of peer educators and volunteers in the classroom are all geared to respond to the needs of the students and to help them to avoid failure, or to turn their failures into learning experiences. Such small gestures on the part of the teacher or volunteer as asking to see the students' report cards are very important to these students. Discuss with them any failing or near failing grades and make a serious attempt to assist them in arranging for tutoring, keeping an assignment notebook, learning how to take notes, or learning how to study. *Simply showing them that someone cares* is extremely important. For many of these students, you may be the only person in their lives who demonstrates concern for them. Incredible and sad as this may seem, the fact is that it is quite true.

An important thing to keep in mind while you show them that you care, is that *you must teach them to accept personal responsibility for their own progress.* If they are to become self-directed independent learners and succeed in the real world, they must learn to be personally responsible.

## INSTITUTE PEER COUNSELING

Another strategy for building self-esteem and for getting students to really "buy into" the program is to select some students (two for each class period) to return the following year as lab assistants. Lab assistants assist new students with the computers and with getting the programs onto the screen. They undo paper jams in the printer, pass out materials, take items to the Xerox room, deliver things to the office for the teacher, type on occasion for the teacher, sit and assist other students one on one to proofread their essays and edit them, assist ESL students with English translation, give tours of the lab to visiting guests, sometimes answer the lab telephone, check students' essays, and perform other tasks on request of the teacher.

Students love to serve as Lab Assistants. If possible, provide them with badges or pins which say "Lab Assistant" as this makes them feel important. It has been my experience that student lab assistants/peer educators take the task very seriously and tend to be protective of the lab and the equipment. For example, they are sometimes harder on any students who do not take proper care of the equipment than even a teacher might be.

Lab Assistants provide you with two extra pairs of eyes, ears, hands, and legs, and free you up to provide even more one on one time with the students. In addition, serving as a lab assistant makes the student feel valuable and worthwhile and does a great deal to improve self-confidence and self-esteem. The students look to the lab assistants (peer counselors) as role models, and the lab assistants develop high self-esteem from the role in which they are placed.

## PROVIDE COOPERATIVE LEARNING OPPORTUNITIES

This will be discussed in depth in the succeeding chapter, and will therefore not be covered at this point.

## REDUCE CLASS SIZE OR STUDENT-ADULT RATIOS

In order to meet the needs of these students, as not only teacher, but also as extended family and support person, it is vitally important to limit the class size to just fifteen students. Indeed, the ideal class size for this course is 15 students. By including adult volunteers in the classroom, it is possible to reduce the student-adult ratio.

Another method of building self-esteem is to institute a grading policy of awarding grades on the basis of attitude, effort, and attendance. *Success breeds success*, and once these students, who have never seen grades above B in their lives suddenly see an A or B on their report cards, it will motivate them to work harder not only in this class, but in their other classes.

*Educators must be careful not to make the false assumption that because a student is reading way below grade level and is a potential dropout, that he or she does not have high academic potential.* Once these students manage to raise their reading levels and to experience some success and develop some self-esteem and self-confidence, many of them are able to achieve extremely well academically in all subject areas.

At-risk students comprise nearly 50% of our entire K-12 student population in the U. S. today. Like it or not, they are the future workforce. They are going to be taking care of us in hospitals and medical care facilities. They will be repairing the brakes and engines of our automobiles, and performing maintenance on our commercial aircraft, or perhaps even piloting them. They will be defending our country in the Armed Forces. *They* will be paying *our* Social Security. In short, they are our future.

It would be detrimental and foolhardy to them, to us, and to our country to sell them short. They *can* and *will* perform to their potential if we, in education, give them the extra support they need. Keep in mind that these students are entering the schools with some pretty heavy emotional baggage and with a deficit of self-esteem. All of these things are obstacles to learning, so if we are to expect them to succeed, we cannot plug them into the traditional classroom setting, place them into straight rows, require them to be silent for six hours, and teach them algebra, grammar, or physics.

There is some controversy over the teaching of self-esteem. Teaching students to develop self-esteem should go beyond having them feel good about themselves and should include teaching them that they are worthwhile persons and that what they think, say, and do is important. Although some educators regard the report of the California Task Force to Promote Self-Esteem and Personal and Social Responsibility as too superficial and simplistic a solution, the recommendations of the Task Force discussed in this chapter, if applied with some depth, do improve students' self-perceptions and do cause them to understand that their opinions, statements, and actions do count.

Self-esteem is an essential prerequisite to learning. Therefore, in order for any program for at-risk students to be effective, it must promote and nurture the growth of self-esteem.

# 3

# Cooperative Learning

*People who just do what they are*
*told will always work for people*
*who know why they do it.*

—Dr. Harry Wong

**COOPERATIVE LEARNING WILL BE A** major component of this course curriculum for several reasons. Since the classroom is organized as a professional office environment, the idea of cooperative learning fits perfectly in this course. Employees in the workplace must learn to work together in teams or departments. Interpersonal skills are a must in today's employment arena. Cooperative learning teaches not only academic skills, but also social skills vital for success in the workplace. Also, cooperative learning helps to build students' self-esteem, as stated in the preceding chapter.

Cooperative learning offers some genuine hope in response to the rather dismal statistic that of all the people who lose their first job after completing school, 84% lose the job not because of their inability to perform the job, but because of their inability to get along with people.

In addition, research over the past 50 years, with all types of populations, all ages, in all parts of the world indicates that cooperative learning results in the following: Higher achievement, more time on task, more active participation on the part of students, more talk time (paraphrasing concepts), retention, higher level thinking (bonding leads to acceptance of divergent thinking). Also, students are motivated and want to achieve. Discipline problems decrease. Attendance increases; the drop-out rate decreases; and self-esteem increases. Through the acquisition of social skills, positive peer friendships and constructive peer relationships are formed. These skills are applicable to home, school, the job world, and to culture. There are *five principles of cooperative learning.* These are:

1. Distributed Leadership
2. Heterogeneous Grouping
3. Positive Interdependence
4. Social Skills Acquisition
5. Group Autonomy

## DISTRIBUTED LEADERSHIP

Distributed leadership involves the sharing of leadership by giving each student in the group a role. There is no one leader, and everyone plays an important role in the completion of the goal or project. (Sample roles might be: facilitator, reporter, recorder, parliamentarian, checker, materials person, etc.)

The role of the teacher involves interacting rather than the conventional role of intervening. In this course, the role of the teacher is that of manager, not teacher, and this is a natural extension of that role.

## HETEROGENEOUS GROUPING

Heterogeneous grouping is an important principle of cooperative learning, and it is vital that the teacher select the groups and include a mixture of abilities, sexes, ages, ethnic groups, and students from different cliques.

Group size should be limited to 3 and groups should be rotated upon completion of each project so that all students get the opportunity to work with all other students in the class at one time or another.

## POSITIVE INTERDEPENDENCE

Positive interdependence is achieved through having students share materials while they assume individual accountability for their respective assignments as part of the group assignment or project. In addition, each student in the group is given an important role; there are no leaders or followers. Everyone is made to feel that his or her contribution is important toward the success of the group and the completion of the one goal or project of the group. This forces the group members to become interdependent in a positive manner since they all need one another in order to accomplish the goal or project.

Rewards are an important, but not required factor in positive interdependence. For example, if everyone in the group earns at least a particular score on a test, or if everyone in the group meets some criteria of success specified by the teacher, the group earns bonus points.

It is important to emphasize that *with cooperative learning, one's grade can only go up.* This is quite different from the traditional concept of "working in groups" in which one student's grade might suffer if he did all of the work and others in the group did not do their parts.

## SOCIAL SKILLS ACQUISITION

Social Skills Acquisition is taught using the following procedure:

1. Define and provide rationale for the skill.
2. Describe how to perform the skill.
3. Practice how to perform the skill.
4. Receive feedback on performance of the skill.
5. Process learnings about the use of the skill.
6. Continue practice until the skill is automatic.

While observing the groups using social skills, the teacher should:

1. Clearly describe the behavior observed.
2. Avoid evaluating the person doing the behavior.
3. State the effect the behavior has on the situation.
4. Refrain from comparing people or groups.

Use a T-chart to show students what a social skill looks like and what it sounds like. For example:

### Encourage Others

| *Sounds Like* | *Looks Like* |
|---|---|
| We can do it. Let's go! | Pat on the back. |
| Keep after them. | Smile approvingly. |
| Let's try again. | Eye contact. |
| Good job! | Thumbs up. |

Write the T-chart on a large sheet of paper and save it for the next time you teach this skill, take out the paper with the T-chart and hang it up on the board. (Dishon and O'Leary, 42–56)

Social skills may be divided into two types: *Task skills* are necessary for completion of the task assigned. *Maintenance skills* are skills which are necessary for the group to work together effectively. Examples of both of these types of skills include the following.

### Task Skills

Check others' understanding of the work.
Give information and opinions.
Stay on task.
Encouragement.
Get group back to work.
Paraphrase.
Seek information and opinions.
Follow directions.

### Maintenance Skills

Encourage.
Use names.
Encourage others to talk.
Eye contact.
Acknowledge contributions.
Express appreciation.
Share feelings.
Disagree in an agreeable way.
Reduce tension.
Practice active listening.
Respond to ideas.

It is important to have *two noise signals to alert students to either lower their noise volume or to have absolute quiet. A possible signal for absolute quiet might be to turn the room lights off and on once or twice. A signal for lowering the volume might be to raise your hand and put up your index finger. Teach students to follow suit by raising their own hands in such a manner when they see you in order to indicate that they are aware of your message to lower the volume.*

Show them that noise is a continuum, with **0** being a whisper and **15** being a yell. A noise level of about **3** is appropriate for cooperative learning groups' discussions. Have them practice what a level-3 noise sounds like. Also, use *color cards* (e.g., yellow cards) to indicate that the noise level in a group is too loud, and that they need to lower the volume. When you place a yellow card on a group's table or work area, it is their responsibility to take steps to lower the noise level. If they do not do so, then use disciplinary measures to ensure that they do.

## GROUP AUTONOMY

Group autonomy is important in making cooperative learning work. The teacher must allow the group to work out its own problems if at all possible. Do not intervene in the group's affairs unless students are having difficulty and ask for your help. If a group is having difficulty working together, don't solve their problems for them. Ask them such questions as: What does your group think? What have you tried so far?

## PROCESSING

Processing involves thinking about how a task was achieved. There are 3 types of processing: analysis, application, and goal setting. *Analysis* means that all responses deal with the group experience just completed. *Application* deals with what students learned from this group experience that could be applied to other situations. *Goal setting* gives students an opportunity to choose a specific social skill to use more efficiently at the next cooperative group session.

When you are observing the groups, avoid saying, "good" or "excellent." Merely say, "I saw."

Cooperative learning will add a valuable new dimension to this course curriculum, and should help students to be better prepared to succeed in the workplace.

## INTRODUCTORY COOPERATIVE LEARNING ACTIVITIES

The following pages contain a few sample cooperative learning activities to use in introducing students to the concept of cooperative learning. It is important for them to understand the principles of cooperative learning and the value of it to them in their lives as future members of the workforce and as contributing citizens in the community.

The first five pages are sample handouts for students for the first day of school. The purpose of these is to get them curious about cooperative learning and to begin their year on a positive, caring note.

The first handout intentionally requires that they must ask another student if they have questions, and may not ask the teacher. The goal is to get them to become interdependent and tot begin to build their interpersonal skills.

The individual teacher should tailor these handouts to meet his or her needs and the needs of the students. It might be a good idea to have the students decide upon names for their respective departments and to decide upon duties or responsibilities of those departments with respect to the office (classroom). For instance, the personnel department might acknowledge students on birthdays with cards or banners, or might award *peer approval certificates* when individual students achieve wonderful things.

# HI THERE!
## WELCOME TO _____ENGLISH.
### I'M REALLY GLAD YOU'RE HERE

*First Day Instructions*

Please complete the following directions. After you have completed each task, place your initials on the appropriate blank line, indicating that you have done what the directions have asked you to do. If you do not understand the directions, you may ask anyone *except* the teacher for help. GOOD LUCK!

_____ 1. The name plate you have been given has inside it the number of the desk you have been assigned to. Please sit at that desk and place your name plate on your desk.

_____ 2. Also inside the name plate are the desk numbers of the others in your learning group. Please introduce yourself to those people. Be sure to know their first names.

_____ 3. You have also been give a Student Information Sheet. Please complete the sheet.

_____ 4. Read the following rules for this class:

   A. Every day you need to bring to class a pen or pencil and a notebook for taking notes.

   B. No food or drink is permitted in this lab, and you are expected and are responsible for taking proper care of the equipment.

   C. We will be using two *noise signals* in the class which you will be required to learn and abide by.

**IT'S GOING TO BE A GREAT YEAR.**
**I'M GLAD YOU'RE HERE.**

# I WANT YOU!
## TO BE SUCCESSFUL

In this course, you will learn how to work with others as you would in a department or office in the employment arena. We will engage in a great deal of *cooperative learning* which will teach you academic skills as well as social and interpersonal skills which are vital in the workplace.

Statistics show that over 80% of people who lose their first job after they complete school lose their jobs not because they cannot do the jobs, but because they cannot get along with other people.

You will be assigned to groups which will change for each project you complete. During the year you will have the chance to work with everyone in the class. If you are not happy with your group, I want you to try to say only positive things about them. You don't have to live with the group, only work with them.

*Each student will be graded individually*, and in addition if your group meets certain criteria specified by me (e.g., if everyone int he group earns at least a 90% on a quiz), your group will receive *additional bonus points* which may be used for a variety of privileges of fun things throughout the year. Thus, *your grade can only go up* as a result of cooperative learning.

Each person in the group will have an important role to play and each person's contribution will be important to the success of the group.

# STUDENT INFORMATION SHEET

Name _____
             (last name)                           (first name)

Student ID # _____ Grade Level _____

Date of birth _____

Address _____

_____

Phone Number_____

    What career are you interested in learning about in order to pursue that career after high school?

    List your subjects for this semester and your teacher in the spaces below.

Period 1 _____

Period 2 _____

Period 3 _____

Period 4 _____

Period 5 _____

Period 6 _____

Are you employed? _____

    If so, how many hours a week do you work?_____

    What is the one thing you want to learn in English this year?

*Introductory Cooperative Learning Activity*

### SQUARES AND TRIANGLES

Give the students the page with the squares and tell them they have three minutes to count the squares. They many not communicate with anyone, and if they finish early, they may fill out the bottom of the page.

After three minutes, call on several of them and ask how many squares they found on the page. Then tell them to correct number (40) and show them on a transparency how to count them. Ask them how they felt during the three minutes.

Their responses to this segment of the activity will generally indicate a high level of anxiety and obvious feelings of uncertainty and insecurity. They will probably indicate that they felt pressured by time constraints and by the curiosity to know if their answers were the same as those of other students. Also, they might indicate that they were not exactly sure of how to go about counting the various squares.

Now give them the large triangle and tell them they have three minutes to count the triangles. Again, they may not talk. After three minutes show them on transparency how to count the 25 triangles. Ask them how they felt during the three minutes.

Again, they will probably express some of the same reservations or feelings of anxiety as they did after the segment with the squares. This time their level of anxiety will decrease slightly as a result of the fact that they have already counted the squares and have been shown by the teacher how to count them.

Finally, give them the small triangle and have them work in groups of three to count the triangles. This time they are to ensure that every member of the group can count the number they agree upon, and then they are to sign the sheet to signify that this is the case. Also, the signatures indicate that everyone in the group can explain to the class how to count these. They have *five* minutes this time.

After five minutes, ask how many each group counted, and tell them that there are 15. Collect the signed pages. Ask them how they felt this time.

At this point, their responses undoubtedly will be much different from the previous responses. They will probably indicate that they felt much more at ease and more secure working with others and teaching one another how to count the triangles.

Ask them whether they prefer to work alone as they did the first time, or in a small group as they did this time. Their responses will very likely indicate that they found the group work much more pleasant and less threatening. At this point, it is an opportune time to discuss with them what cooperative learning is and go over the benefits of it for them as students.

It is a good idea to use cooperative learning about one third to one half of the time. It is not wise to use it to the total exclusion of individual work. Students need to learn to work as independent, self-directed learners as well as team members.

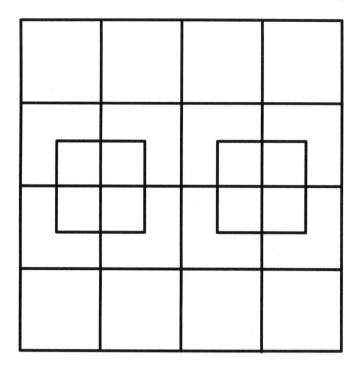

**How Did I Feel?**

**What Did I Notice?**

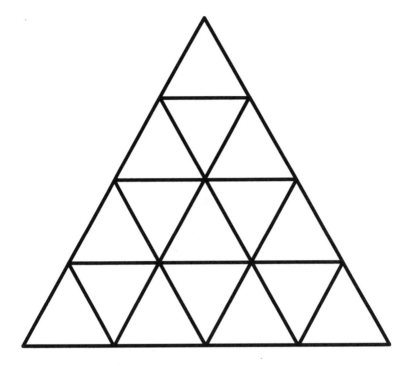

**How Did I Feel?**

**What Did I Notice?**

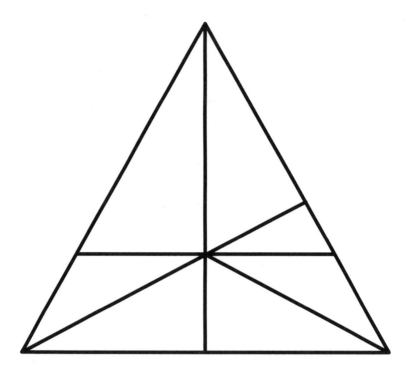

**How Did I Feel?**

**What Did I Notice?**

## FRACTURED RECTANGLES

*Format*: Each person in the group receives an envelope with parts from different broken rectangles. The groups are told:

Your task is to form a rectangle for each individual, using these rules:

1. You may not speak.

2. You may not use nonverbal signs to ask anyone for a part.

3. You can give parts to others.

Each individual must end up with one rectangle the same size as everyone else's rectangles.

*Materials*: The rectangles are broken and distributed as follows:

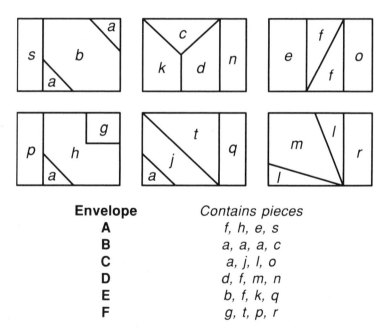

| Envelope | Contains pieces |
|----------|-----------------|
| A | f, h, e, s |
| B | a, a, a, c |
| C | a, j, l, o |
| D | d, f, m, n |
| E | b, f, k, q |
| F | g, t, p, r |

# 4

# Reading Comprehension—A Whole Language Approach

## THE SCOPE OF THE PROBLEM OF ILLITERACY IN THE U.S.

"LET US DARE TO READ, to write to speak, to think..." President John Adams spoke these words to emphasize the vital role of literacy in a democratic society ("Unlocking the Future," 1). Democracy, by its very nature, depends upon a literate, educated electorate to make informed judgements about candidates for public office and about issues facing the nation. Noted educator, Dr. John Henry Martin, summed it up this way: "Literacy may not guarantee freedom, but illiteracy will promote its death" (Martin, 1986, p.6).

Ironically, after two hundred years of commitment to this ideal, illiteracy has become one of the most critical issues facing the United States in this decade. National polls and surveys indicate that there are now an estimated 50 million illiterate adults in the United States and an additional 39 million who have great difficulty with reading (Lavin & Sanders, 68). The situation shows little hope of improving, since there is an estimated increase of two million in the number of functional illiterates in this country every year.

Illiteracy in the workplace has become a major issue of the 90's and many companies are instituting their own workplace literacy programs for their employees. Today, as the workplace becomes increasingly complex and as new management styles and technologies are implemented, companies are finding it more and more difficult to find qualified workers to handle these new jobs. This situation is projected to become even worse in the next decade. A harsh reality facing American workers today is that jobs that cannot be filled by skilled U.S. workers will be filled with foreigners. Consequently, our students are competing not only with their peers, they are competing with the best students from West Germany, Japan, and other countries.

At the root of the problem of illiteracy in the workplace is the fact that the national dropout rate is a startling 30%. In urban schools, the dropout rate is over 50%. These statistics are indicative of the fact that our current educational system is not adequately preparing all of our students to lead productive lives and that the United States itself may soon be at-risk if our future workers continue to fail to meet the requirements of the workplace ("Technology and the At-Risk Student" 35).

## THE WHOLE LANGUAGE APPROACH TO TEACHING READING

The whole language approach was developed by educators in response to the need for an alternative approach to the traditional approach which is not working for the majority of our students today. Whole language is a philosophy which emphasizes that language should be kept whole and uncontrived and that students should use language in ways that are relevant to their own lives and cultures. This approach emphasizes the process by which the correct answer is found, rather than emphasizing the correct answer itself. In other words, it stresses that the important thing is for students to understand how to arrive at the answer, and to learn to think for themselves, rather than for them to simply memorize the correct answer, with no comprehension of what it means.

The whole language classroom is student-centered. Because students are able to perceive that the material they are learning is meaningful to their lives in the real world, they find the class enjoyable. The teacher is a guide or facilitator, rather than an authoritarian figure in this classroom setting.

Students engage in teaching one another in such a classroom, and cooperative learning is stressed. Some other common techniques used in whole language classrooms include keeping a daily personal journal, letter writing, writing about literature, publishing real student writing, silent or free reading, and oral reading of real literature (Gursky, 22–27).

In classrooms that employ the whole language philosophy, students learn by actively participating in activities that are meaningful to them and by sharing their knowledge with other students. This is in sharp contrast to the traditional classroom in which students were passive participants who took notes and simply acted as sponges to absorb the knowledge imparted by the teacher through lectures.

In short, the whole language approach empowers teachers to be professionals who have the power to design their classrooms and to select the materials and vehicles by which their students will learn. The whole language approach *works*. Moreover, the whole language approach is in agreement with the research on motivational instructional strategies for at-risk students and for building self-esteem.

## TEACHING READING COMPREHENSION WITH COMPUTERS

Computers are one highly effective means of teaching reading comprehension because they are non-threatening to students; they permit students to progress at their own pace; they allow them to repeat the material if they need to do so; and they free the teacher so that he or she is able to provide one on one attention to the students.

Also, most students enjoy working on computers. At-risk students, in particular, who generally lack self-confidence and self-esteem, seem to derive a sense of self-respect and confidence and of great accomplishment from working at computers.

Moreover, there are some excellent reading comprehension software packages designed especially for at-risk students. One such package is *Reading Realities*, by Dr. Shelley B. Wepner and Dr. George E. Mason, published by Teacher Support Software. This whole language software was developed specifically for teens who are reading at the 2nd-6th grade levels. This series includes three highly effective packages, designed to help at-risk students become better readers, writers, and thinkers.

*Real Life Issues*. This package deals with 15 real life issues facing teenagers, such as alcohol dilemma, drugs, teen pregnancy, cheating, dropping out, shop-lifting, child abuse, suicide, living with a handicap.

*Career Preparation*. This package contains biographies which provide information on how to prepare for a variety of careers such as secretary, computer programmer, lawyer, doctor, teacher, pilot, interior designer, hairdresser, sportscaster, photographer, and more.

*Jury Series*. This includes actual trials and the student assumes the role of juror in cases involving drunk driving, possession of drugs, murder, stealing, manslaughter, arson, sports tampering, etc.

Each package has 15 stories which involve students' active participation in reading comprehension and creative writing as well as in writing answers to discussion questions. At the start of each passage, there is a preview of vocabulary for that passage. Each passage is also followed by multiple choice and fill in the blank (cloze) questions. These questions and the student's answers may be printed out together with the scores they earn for each section. Also, the written answers to the essay questions may be printed out to be passed in.

Each of the three segments of *Reading Realities* comes in a looseleaf binder with a wealth of practical information for the teacher as well as with a myriad of creative activities to employ in the classroom with students. These activities include writing assignments, vocabulary development activities and brainstorming suggestions.

This program is one of the best things that has happened to at-risk students in literacy programs. Students love the program because they find the topics extremely appealing and of interest to them. The text is written at their reading level, but is presented in a mature manner, and aimed at teenagers.

The questions are thought-provoking and relevant to these teens as they deal with the actual real life issues they face daily.

The program guides their thought process through the use of graphics, questions that ask the students to predict what the story is about, objective questions, and discussion and creative questions requiring essay answers. The student's understanding of the text is monitored closely through the placement of questions before and after students read the text.

The program also provides teachers with a management system for seeing all aspects of student progress as individuals or as a class.

*Reading Realities* earned the 1989-90 Classroom Computer Learning Software Award for Excellence — Top Five, **and** the Media & Methods Awards Honoree for Excellence in Education, 1990. For further information, contact:

Teacher Support Software
1035 N.W. 57th St.
Gainesville, FL 32605 - 4483
(904) 332 -6404
(800) 228-2871
FAX: (904) 332 - 6779

Another excellent software package for teaching reading comprehension is the *Reading for Meaning* series by IBM (Levels 1,2,3,4). This program is excellent for use with at-risk students whose reading levels are considerably below grade level. In this program, students are asked to read paragraphs and answer questions. They are also required to dig for meaning and draw inferences.

In addition, the *Reading for Information* series by IBM (Levels 2,3,4) is also excellent for use with these students. This series includes reading and interpreting graphs, charts, diagrams and also reading arguments. The reading selections span a wide variety of topics of interest to students, including science, health, biology, reading maps, reading checkbook pages, reading theater tickets, interpreting charts and diagrams on geology, meteorology, and many other topics. The section on reading arguments is challenging for students, as they are asked to indicate if the speakers have backed up their arguments correctly. They must be able to distinguish between evidence, claims, opinions, and facts.

Charts for recording scores on the various lessons are provided so that the teacher may monitor the progress of each student. Also, the student is able to monitor his or her own progress and then to progress to the next higher level disk.

Another software series which is extremely effective for improving reading comprehension as well as some research skills is the *Carmen Sandiego* series in which students must act as detectives, using clues to research the whereabouts of suspects and apprehend them. These programs transform students who never crack a book into diligent investigators who enthusiastically search through world atlases and pour over world maps attempting to determine the routes of their suspects.

Furthermore, programs not only improve students' reading comprehension skills, they also teach students a great deal about U.S. and world geography and history as well as various cultures. Three students can work together at one computer on this program, and they generally enjoy using the clues given to locate information in the almanac or atlas provided and then applying this to the crime computer and other components of the program in order to solve the crimes cooperatively.

In addition, these *Carmen Sandiego* programs are highly motivational, and they may be used as rewards to be available to students only after the students' work is completed. These programs can be obtained from:

Broderbund
17 Paul Drive,
San Rafael, CA 94903-2102

The cost of each of these programs is generally under $50. Thus, for a rather minimal investment, a greatly effective reading comprehension program may be obtained.

It is a good idea to complement these programs with a framed map of the world hanging on the wall or bulletin board. I have mounted a laminated world map on a bulletin board and have found that students using these programs frequently independently consult the world map to verify their conclusions. They have learned on their own to compare sources and to synthesize the information and draw conclusions or inferences.

## THE NEWSPAPER AND TEACHING READING COMPREHENSION

Another vitally important, and inexpensive tool for improving reading comprehension is the daily newspaper. Encourage your students to read the newspaper daily, and as often as possible, incorporate current events into your writing assignments. Emphasize the importance of being an informed citizen as a voter and active participant in making democracy work. Discuss with the students why this is so important to us and to our country, and talk with them about the consequences of becoming an uninformed, apathetic society. Try to cite examples which are relevant to them in order to illustrate this concept.

It has been my observation that students actually develop greater self-esteem once they start reading the newspaper and become able to discuss current events on a regular basis.

If the local newspaper is too costly or too difficult for the students to read, a very effective alternative is the student publication, *News for You*, published by New Reader's Press (P.O. Box 131, Syracuse, NY 13210). This high-interest-low-vocabulary newspaper is published weekly, and you may receive ten copies per week for a semester, for under $50. The newspaper includes major news stories, feature stories, sports stories, crossword puzzles, and cartoons. Students find the publication appealing, and interesting, while written at their vocabulary level.

## READING REAL LITERATURE

In line with the philosophy of whole language instruction, select some literary pieces which are appropriate for at-risk students with lower reading levels. These selections should be in keeping with any reading requirements of your respective English department or district, and will also be influenced by availability of books at your school. Also, the librarian should be able to reserve a selection of appropriate books in the library for your students. Should you purchase any of the *Reading Realities* Software packages discussed earlier, they all come equipped with a reading list of suggested books for at-risk students.

### Plays

It has been my experience that at-risk students thoroughly enjoy reading the plays *Romeo and Juliet* and *West Side Story*, and that they experience a great sense of accomplishment once they have completed these. Teaching these two plays is not a very easy task, but it is well worth the challenge to see these students beam with great pride and delight in themselves once the unit is completed. In the case of *Romeo and Juliet*, the teacher must read and act the majority of the play. It is possible to read the major scenes, omit some of the more difficult scenes, and still give students the major points of the story. This is a love story with which they are easily able to relate. Upon concluding reading the play, show them the motion picture of the play.

Teaching *West Side Story* is not quite as challenging, as the students will be able to read the parts aloud, and they enjoy doing so. You will probably be surprised to find that while the students may have some difficulty with the reading level at which these plays are written, they will have a keen perception of the characters and human nature involved in these stories. Also, they will have strong opinions about Romeo and Juliet's and Tony and Maria's actions and will relate to these characters quite easily. Again, on completion of reading the play, show them the film of the play on television.

The following pages provide some ideas for activities and writing assignments to employ for teaching this unit.

**Essay Assignment:**

Have the students write an essay comparing and contrasting these two plays. As a prewriting exercise, discuss with them in what ways the plays are similar and in what ways they are quite different. Also, discuss how one might compare and contrast the main characters of the two plays. Also, discuss how one might logically organize the content of this essay, and have them make a rough outline of paragraphing to use as a guide for themselves while writing their papers.

Worksheet ROMEO AND JULIET

Name _____

Answer the questions below in complete sentences.

1. Explain in 2 or 3 sentences what is meant by "star-crossed lovers."

2. Why are Romeo and Juliet star-crossed lovers?

3. Explain how Romeo meets Juliet. What events led up to their meeting?

4. Describe the balcony scene in 4 or 5 sentences. This is probably the most famous love scene in all literature.

5. Explain the meaning of the lines: "What's in a name? That which we call a rose by any other name would smell as sweet."

6. Who is Tybalt? How does he cause difficulties for Romeo and Juliet?

7. The nurse is the comic character in the play. Describe her personality.

8. What does Romeo say about Juliet's eyes and cheeks that relates to light or brightness?

9. This play is one of Shakespeare's tragedies. What is a tragedy?

10. Explain what does Juliet mean by the line, "My only love sprung from my only hate! Too early seen unknown and known too late!"

## Discussion and Essay Topic

Discuss whether or not the students feel that Romeo and Juliet were justified in taking their own lives. Let the discussion serve as prewriting, and have them write an argument supporting their position.

### Simulation

Have them play roles and simulate the scene in which Juliet goes to Friar Lawrence for his advice and assistance. If you were Friar Lawrence, what advice would you have given Juliet?

### Talk Show

Have a talk show in which the guests are William Shakespeare, Romeo, Juliet, Friar Lawrence and Paris. Have students volunteer to play these parts, and have the other students serve as the audience. The audience must write a question for each guest. These are then given to the host, who asks them of the guests. The students playing the roles of the guest characters must answer the questions as they feel the character they are playing would have answered them.

### Writing Assignment

Have the girls write a journal or diary which Juliet might have written from the time she met Romeo until her untimely death. Have the boys write Romeo's journal for the same time period until his own untimely death. As a prewriting exercise have them brainstorm the types of things that they might have included in their journals.

### Romeo and Juliet of the 1990s

Work in groups and complete this writing assignment as a cooperative learning activity. Have them write a 1990s version of this story of Romeo and Juliet. If this is successful, have them read these or discuss these with the class.

## Poetry

Another genre of literature which is quite effective with at-risk students is poetry. Students will protest vociferously about having to read poetry; yet they will frequently spend time on their own writing poetry. As part of a unit of study on poetry, assign the students to write poems of their own, and undoubtedly some students will ask if they may pass in poems they have already written for extra credit.

Poetry ignites their creativity and inspires their imagination. It also requires them to employ some higher level thinking skills to comprehend and apply such concepts as metaphor or irony. Begin the unit with an introduction to the difference between literal language and figurative language, which, of course, is the substance of poetry.

Use the following cooperative learning activity in order to get the students to teach one another these concepts of figures of speech. Have them also try to write original examples of these.

As mentioned in the discussion on teaching *Romeo and Juliet* and *West Side Story*, at-risk students derive a great sense of achievement from learning advanced concepts, and from acquiring sophisticated vocabulary words which they are then able to use.

In addition, research shows that students' achievement is greater when teachers set high levels of expectations for their students. Let the students know that you are confident that they can achieve the requirements and outcomes you set for them, and that you will help them as much as possible to ensure that they will succeed.

*Cooperative Learning Activity*

## FIGURES OF SPEECH

### Implementation

Students will work in small heterogeneous groups to learn a list of figures of speech and their definitions, as an introduction to a unit on poetry and figurative language. They will quiz one another to ensure that everyone in the group knows these well enough to identify them and to pass a test successfully on them. They will sign the study page in order to indicate that they know all of these figures of speech. They will then be given a test on another day, and if everyone in the group earns at least an 80% on the test, the group will earn 500 bonus points and will be rewarded by being able to watch a movie on Friday.

There will be distributed leadership as the students will assume the roles of *recorder / facilitator, encourager,* and *parliamentarian.* Individual accountability will be accomplished because each student's test will be graded individually.

### Social Skill Instruction

The social skill of *encouragement* will be taught by use of a T-chart because it will be important to make sure that they all understand the figures of speech and feel confident that they can identify them in lines of poetry.

### Process

Students will be asked to talk among themselves and process how they learned the figures of speech. Did they have some memory devices or some method of grouping them (e.g., simile and metaphor; personification and apostrophe)? They will be asked to share this briefly with the class.

They will complete the statement: In any group it is helpful to _____and _____because _____.

The encourager will be asked to share these answers with the class.

## FIGURES OF SPEECH

**alliteration** — repetition of initial sounds of words in a row. (Peter Piper picked a peck of pickled peppers.)

**allusion** — reference to a famous person or event from history or literature. (That was his Waterloo.)

**apostrophe** — speaking to inanimate objects as if they were alive, or speaking to a deceased person as if he were alive. (Oh, car, you've got to start.)

**figurative language** — exaggerated language.

**figures of speech** — examples of figurative language.

**hyperbole** — a vast exaggeration. (His mouth is so big he can whisper in his own ears!)

**irony** — the opposite of what you expect happens.

**literal language** — means exactly what it says.

**metaphor** — same as simile, but not using "like" or "as." (She is an angel.)

**paradox** — apparent contradiction. (The best man for the job is a woman.)

**personification** — giving human qualities to inanimate or inhuman things. (My car told me to clean it.)

**simile** — a comparison of two unlike things, using the words "like" or "as." (She sings like a bird.)

**synecdoche** — the part stands for the whole or the whole for the part. (All hands on deck on the double.)

**symbol** — something that stands for something else. (golden arches stand for McDonald's.)

## SUGGESTED ACTIVITIES

Read some poetry with students and discuss it with them. Have them try to identify the figures of speech and discuss how they add to the effectiveness of the poems.

*****

Poetry is a great release for emotions, and you will find that at-risk students enjoy writing poetry. Encourage them to do so, and concentrate on the content rather than the mechanics of their work.

*****

Sometimes it is fun to have them work in pairs to write poetry. Give them unusual topics to spark their creativity. Some topics might be the following: skateboards, ratty sneakers, algebra, drugs, eyes, computers, being handicapped, pizza, cotton candy, music.

*****

*Essay Assignment:*

Read Robert Frost's poem, "The Road Not Taken," and have them write about a time in their lives when they came to a "fork in the road," and had to make a decision. Ask them to relate it to the poem. Did they choose the easy route or the more difficult, less-traveled one? Has that made a difference in their lives?

## SILENT OR FREE READING

Another whole language strategy which promotes improved reading comprehension skills is the silent or free reading time set aside each day for the purpose of allowing students to select something of interest to them to read. This requires that the classroom be equipped with a lending library stocked with books and magazines of interest to these students. Also, try to have on hand any informational publication (such as the driver's license manual) which has some meaning or relevance to the students' interests or daily lives.

The chapter on writing skills recommends the publication of student writing in the form of a literary magazine. Be sure to have several copies of that publication available for students to read during free reading time. Students love to read one another's writing, and seeing their own names in print helps to boost their self-esteem and encourages them to take pride in their writing and in their work in general.

During the time allotted for free reading, the teacher should also read, setting the tone for the students. Do not sit and correct papers or perform other administrative tasks during this time, as it is vital for the students to perceive that the teacher places a great deal of importance on reading regularly.

## LEARNING STRATEGIES AND READING COMPREHENSION

A highly effective means of helping students to improve their reading comprehension skills is to use learning strategies to teach them methods which will help them to accomplish their goals. These strategies help students to rehearse the learning process and to understand how to arrive at the desired outcome. As mentioned earlier in the discussion on the philosophy of whole language, many students simply memorize material and have no comprehension of the material or of the process by which a correct answer may be found. Learning strategies can bridge that gap for the students and provide the link that they need to truly master the process of learning.

One reading comprehension strategy which I have used with hundreds of students with a high degree of success is the *Paraphrasing Strategy* developed and validated by J.B. Schumaker, P.H. Denton, and D.D. Deshler, at the University of Kansas Institute of Research in Learning Disabilities. This strategy teaches students to read a paragraph at a time and to identify and recall the main idea and specific details. Students practice the strategy two or three times per week using specified readers until they are able to transfer that skill to the reading of their assigned work in their textbooks for all of their classes.

The strategy has the acronym RAP, which stands for *Read* a paragraph; *Ask* yourself what the main ideas and details are in the paragraph; *Put* this information into your own words. The authors of this strategy recommend that anyone wishing to use it should obtain training from the Institute of Research in Learning Disabilities, University of Kansas, Lawrence, Kansas 66045.

### SUMMARY

The great debate over how students learn will probably continue ad infinitum. Although there is general agreement that our traditional school system in this country is not working adequately for the vast majority of our student population, there is not a great deal being done to change that. Most of the proposed school reforms and solutions to repair our failing educational system simply advocate more of the same worn out methods. There are recommendations for extended school days, a lengthened school year, more standardized national testing, increased teacher accountability, better teacher training, and higher academic standards. However, very little has been said in the debate over national school reform with regard to how students learn (Gursky, 29).

Proponents of the whole language philosophy advocate that the national education reform movement refocus its attention on classroom learning and on the whole language theory of literacy which will eventually change the way that teachers teach, and the way that classrooms and schools are organized and run (Gursky, 29).

After almost five years of teaching at-risk students in a special English class, I strongly concur with the whole language advocates that the whole language classroom is much more responsive to the needs of the at-risk students than is the traditional classroom because the curriculum and activities as well as the learning environment are designed to meet the needs and interests of these students.

# 5

# Introduction to the Writing Process

MOTIVATING AT-RISK STUDENTS to learn to improve their writing skills is an area that is extremely challenging. It requires helping students to break a cycle of low expectations and acceptance of failure. Research on the motivation theory of attribution shows that students who have had patterns of failure tend to attribute their failures to certain reasons, such as:

1. Lack of ability ("I just cannot write.")
2. Not employing sufficient effort ("I didn't try very hard. I could do it if I tried.")
3. Task is too difficult ("The work is too hard.")
4. Luck ("I made a lucky guess.")

Students who think this way also consider that they are helpless and cannot succeed. They believe that it is beyond their control to prevent failure or to ensure success. Therefore, it is not enough for them to simply experience success in school. Teachers need to assist them in breaking this cycle of low expectation and helplessness (Alderman, 27).

In order to accomplish this, teachers must have a high sense of their own *efficacy* (confidence in their ability to influence students' learning and motivation). Teachers with a high degree of efficacy consider their students as not only reachable, but capable of high expectation. Teachers must convey to their students that they want them to succeed, and that they will not lower their expectations for their students (Alderman, 28).

However, helping students to experience success is not enough. They must understand how they achieved that success in order that they will be able to see that success is not a product of luck; rather, they have the power to assure themselves success or failure by the actions or strategies they employ in their schoolwork (Alderman, 28).

By using the steps in the writing process, the teacher can help students to improve their writing skills and to understand a systematic progression from the original thought process to transferring that thought into written form on paper.

Begin by assigning an essay topic for the week every Monday and giving the students until Friday to pass in the corrected rough draft, final draft, and *Written Composition Checklist* (included here). Repeat this process every week. The more frequently students write and follow the writing process, the more they will improve in their written composition skills.

In keeping with the office-setting rationale, a suggestion is to hold a weekly office meeting every Monday, during which the week's work (essay topic and any other work to be covered that week) is assigned.

Introduce the topic and spend some time with them on the **prewriting** phase of the writing process. Have them discuss the topic and suggest ideas that one might include in the essay. Discuss types of introductory sentences or paragraphs one might use to begin the essay. Also, discuss types of ways to develop the body of the essay, and possible ways to write a conclusion for the essay. The conclusion might summarize the paper; ask a question; make a strong or shocking statement; tell a short story; include a quote, or include a different method of clinching or ending the paper.

Next, during the **drafting** phase of the writing process, have them go to their work stations, and brainstorm or jot down ideas on paper. They will take turns using the computers and word processing program to begin the first draft. (Information on a word processing program is contained later in the chapter.) While one person in each department uses the computer, the other two will do other work assigned by the teacher at their tables.

Then, during the **editing** phase, they should have a partner proofread and mark their paper for corrections. After the partner checks the paper, the student should edit it himself/herself, and then run the Spell Check through the paper.

If *Writer's Helper* or *Grammatik III* is available in your lab, the student should then use one or both of those programs to check correct grammar and usage. Eventually, they should also check for correct punctuation and good organization. During this revising phase the student prepares the final draft for publishing (the final phase of the writing process). This final draft is passed in stapled to the rough draft (marked with corrections).

In selecting topics to assign for essays, begin with those topics which involve personal writing at first. It is easier for students to write about themselves or about things that relate to them at first.

Then progress to writing a description, and to topics which are mainly creative in nature. Finally, progress to those topics which involve more of the higher level thinking skills, such as persuasive writing, and the essay of opinion.

Included in the next chapter are suggested essay topics and some actual writing lessons which the teacher may employ. It is also important to keep the interests of your respective students in mind, and select topics that will appeal to them. Students tend to become much more motivated to write if the topic is one to which they can relate or one in which they are interested.

Included in this chapter is a sample *Written Composition Checklist*, and a page on suggested software to use for writing assignments. Also, there are some pages on using transitional expressions to improve writing. Students will find these helpful in establishing a smoother transition or better organization in their writing.

# WRITTEN COMPOSITION CHECKLIST

Name _____

Date started _____ Date completed _____

## Prewriting

My partner is _____

Some ideas we discussed were: _____

_____

_____

We completed our prewriting by:

    talking about it _____ making notes on paper_____

## Drafting

Topic of essay _____

Rough Draft Completed_____

## Editing

Draft copy reviewed by (partner)_____

Capitalization checked_____ Punctuation checked _____

Is the content clearly organized? _____

Is there smooth transition between ideas? _____

Spell Check completed _____

Grammar Check completed _____

## Revising

Changes and corrections complete _____

## Publishing

Final revised draft completed _____

Rough draft, final draft, and this form to be stapled together and passed in.

## Using Transitional Expressions to Improve Writing

Provide them with copies of the following page of transitional expressions, and instruct them to use them when they write, and to underline them so that they stand out and I can see that they are using them.

## Topic Sentences

Discuss how to write a good topic sentence and go over types of comments to avoid such as: my paper is about... I am going to write about... the end...

## Using Other's Feedback to Improve Writing

Point out that using other people's responses can help you to shape and develop your writing.

### Listener-oriented

*Pointing*: ("I liked") Listeners just point to things they liked.

*Active listening or sayback*: Listener says, in own words, what he or she hears the writer saying.

*Center of gravity*: ("Your main idea seems to be...") Listener states the main idea succinctly -what he or she hears as the focus or heart of the paper.

### Writer-oriented:

1. What holds this piece together? (What other ideas do you hear? What implicit or explicit supporting points?)

2. What do you want to know more about? (What's said? What needs to be said?)

3. What parts did you like best & why did they strike you?

4. What else could I say? (What needs elaboration?)

5. What am I trying to say? (What's my intention?)

## TRANSITIONAL EXPRESSIONS

Use these to make your ideas flow more smoothly from one paragraph or sentence to the next.

| *Same Idea* | *Opposite Idea* | *Example* |
|---|---|---|
| furthermore | however | for example |
| moreover | nevertheless | for instance |
| also | | |
| in addition | | |
| indeed | *Contrast* | *Result* |
| as a matter of fact | although | consequently |
| additionally | in comparison | therefore |
| similarly | on the other hand | as a result |
| | on the contrary | accordingly |
| | in contrast | |

| *Place* | | |
|---|---|---|
| here | *Time* | *Reason or Purpose* |
| there | when | because |
| near | while | in order to |
| over | meanwhile | for the purpose of |
| far | after | because of |
| in the proximity | now | |
| in the vicinity | finally | |
| | before | |
| | soon | *Conditional* |
| | presently | if |
| | as | granted |
| | eventually | provided |
| | during | |
| | then | |
| | afterward | |

## *Another Method of Transition*

Connect ideas in two sentences by using a word in the second sentence that refers to a word or group of words in the first sentence.

Example: George made some really ludicrous comments during the interview. Not only were his comments ridiculous, but he looked ridiculous with that pair of fake glasses and rubber nose.

## RECOMMENDED SOFTWARE FOR WRITING PROCESS

### Word Processing

*Writing Assistant*

This is a simple, easy to follow word processing program by IBM. It contains a spell check and thesaurus. The program also allows students to move paragraphs around to revise the organization of their papers. Classroom packages are available at an inexpensive price.

### Grammar Checkers

*Writer's Helper*
The University of Iowa
CONDUIT
Oakdale Campus
Iowa City, IA 52242

This program deals with 3 steps in the writing process: prewriting, drafting, revising. Revising Tools allow students to check for errors of usage, and to find structural defects.

*Grammatik III*
Reference Software, Inc.
330 Townsend St., Ste 123
San Francisco, CA 94107

This highly sophisticated program checks students' writing for errors of grammar, usage, punctuation, sentence length, etc. This program may be a bit too complex for these students. Upon completion of grammar check, the program provides an assessment of the writing analyzed, including the grade level at which it is written.

## PUBLICATION OF STUDENTS' WRITING

One strategy for building students' self-esteem and for also motivating them to achieve further is to publish their writing and to celebrate their successes. Therefore, as the year progresses, collect pieces of student writing which are particularly good or which show great improvement on the part of the individual student. Then put together a booklet or literary magazine of these writings and print copies for everyone in the class.

With desktop publishing programs and laser quality printers, it is now possible to produce publications which appear to be professionally printed. This will help students to build pride in their writing and in their achievement.

If possible, include photos in the booklet. With the modern copy machines, it is possible to make copies of color or black and white photos in half-tones for 10 cents per page. Students love to see their writing in print and their photos printed also.

In addition, there are some publications which will publish writing by students. If at all possible, submit your students' writing to one or more of these publications, and let your students enjoy the excitement of being published nationally.

## WRITING ABOUT LITERATURE

Another strategy utilized in whole language classrooms is writing about literature. This is one method of causing students to think about the literature they read. It helps to promote reading comprehension, because one must comprehend the content of the literature in order to write an essay about it.

Utilizing whatever literature is taught in your classroom, design some writing assignments which get students to focus on the themes, characters, or content or issues which are dealt with in the various readings. The assignment might be as simple as asking them to write about what they can learn from the main character in the reading. They might be asked to discuss the theme of the reading and explain how they might apply what they learn from that in their own lives. Another assignment might be to write a different ending for the story they have read.

Also, they might be asked to compare and contrast two characters or two stories. Have them put themselves in the place of someone in the story and tell what they would do if they were in that person's situation.

Writing about the literature also will help them to remember the literature and to develop a better understanding and appreciation of what they read. Mainly, this type of assignment will help students to improve both reading and writing skills.

# 6

# Writing Instruction and Essay Topics

THIS CHAPTER IS INTENDED to provide the teacher of at-risk students with many lesson ideas and opportunities for practical application of the writing process and of the concepts discussed in the previous chapter.

This chapter contains numerous sample writing assignments. These are divided into three sections. The first of these is **Personal Writing**, which includes topics which are relevant to the student personally or to his or her life in the real world. In writing these, students should be encouraged to draw upon their personal warehouses of ideas and experiences.

The second section, **Creative Writing**, contains a wide variety of writing assignments and cooperative learning projects involving writing which require the students to think creatively. The topics included here are derived from areas which are generally of interest to high school students.

The third section, **Persuasive Writing**, focuses on essays of opinion which are intended to be persuasive or to present the student's opinions or convictions, well substantiated by solid reasons. This type of writing causes students to employ higher level thinking skills such as synthesis, analysis, and evaluation.

## TEACHER FEEDBACK FOR STUDENT WRITING

In order to promote success for students in the development and improvement of writing skills, it is crucial that the teacher give students some specific feedback and some positive, encouraging comments on their papers. Simply placing a letter grade on the paper serves no instructional value and does nothing to encourage that student to do better next time. Make a few comments about the content and organization, for starters, and show them how to use the spell checker on the word-processing program you are using.

After a couple of months of weekly writing assignments, teach them to use grammar checker and usage checker software.

Conversely, since most at-risk students have poor writing skills, it is also important that the teacher not bleed red ink all over the students' papers, thereby overwhelming and intimidating them from ever trying to write and share their writing with an audience of readers in the future.

As they write more and more frequently and more systematically, following the steps of the writing process, with peer editing and feedback, and using spell, grammar, and usage checkers, they will improve in the clarity, organization, and actual content of their written expression.

## PERSONAL WRITING

### Journal Writing

Throughout the year it is also a good idea to have students keep a personal journal. The journal should be a special safe place where students may express themselves and voice their most personal feelings without the anxiety of teacher scrutiny or grades. Have them write in their journals once or twice a week.

Also, tell them to write down any creative or original ideas they have which they might wish to incorporate into an essay at a later date. It is a good idea to write these ideas down in a separate section of the journal so that they might easily locate them at times when they wish to use them in their writing assignments.

Collect their journals once a week and write comments, but do not grade them. Often students will use the journal as a vehicle to communicate their concerns to the teacher. Assure them that their journals are confidential and will not be shared with anyone else, unless there is any information included of a criminal nature which you must report to authorities, or unless they mention substance abuse problems in which case you will try to get them referred for help.

Journal writing is a strategy used widely in whole language classrooms. An important benefit of journal writing is that it allows students the freedom of written expression without a prescribed topic or structured guidelines.

## Essay Assignments:

## What Type of Parent Will You Be?

Write an essay about the type of parent you plan to be someday. Include a discussion of the types of rules you will have and the manner in which you plan to bring up your family.

*Pre-writing*: Help them to get started by asking them to make a list on scratch paper of the things they will do and the things they won't do when they become parents someday. Discuss how to organize them so that they will be in a logical, cohesive order. Go over how to use transitional expressions to link these ideas together in a smooth manner.

Have them follow the rest of the steps in the writing process and produce a rough draft which will be proofread and corrected by a partner, and then edited and revised and a final draft eventually written.

## Letter to A Newborn Baby

Write a letter to a newborn baby giving him or her advice on growing up in today's world. Share your years of wisdom with the newborn. Tell him/her what you've learned over the years, and what experiences have been valuable learning experiences for you. Give the baby advice on getting along with people, getting ahead in life, acquiring an education, etc. Ask them what advice they would have for a newborn baby about life. Have them follow the steps of the writing process, and use the checklists to check their grammar, punctuation, spelling, organization, etc.

## Prejudice

What does the word *prejudice* mean to you? Do you feel you have any prejudices toward other people? Why is prejudice a destructive feeling? Have you ever experienced prejudice? Write an essay on this topic.

## Goals

What are your goals for yourself in life? What do you hope to accomplish as an adult? What career do you think you'd be interested in pursuing? What training or preparation will you need for that career? Write an essay on this topic.

## If you could speak to anyone in the world for one hour...

If you could speak to anyone in the world for one hour, to whom would you want to speak, and why would you want to speak to that person? What questions would you ask that person? What things would you want to say to that person? What would you expect to gain from this experience? Would you learn anything important? Would you accomplish anything significant? Write an essay that answers these questions in complete detail. Be sure your topics are organized in a logical, clear manner and that you have an introductory sentence and a conclusion.

## Person who has influenced you the most

Write an essay discussing the person who has had the greatest positive influence on you. What relationship is this person to you, if any? In what ways has this person influenced you? How have you changed as a person as a result of this person's influence? Be sure to organize your thoughts logically and to include a topic sentence and a conclusion.

## Life in the USA

Write a description of life in the USA for a person living in Russia who has never been to the USA. This should be well organized by specific subtopics (e.g., housing, recreation, daily routine, schools, economy, etc).

## You Build It

If you had $100,000,000 and 100 acres of land, what would you build? Be sure to give a detailed description of your building and what it would be used for in your essay.

## Favorite Place

Write an essay describing the one place in the world you would most like to live for a year. Why would you like to live there? What makes it a special place to you?

## Room Without Windows

In a well organized, well developed essay, answer the following question: If you had to live for one year in a 12-foot square room with no windows, what would you put in it? Why would you put these particular things in it?

## Drinking and Driving

Drinking and driving are a deadly combination. What do you feel would be an appropriate punishment for anyone convicted of driving under the influence of alcohol? It should be a punishment that would really be an effective deterrent to convince people to not drive drunk.

## Self Pride

What was something you did that made you really feel good, and made you really feel proud of yourself? Describe the situation and give specific details in an essay.

## Friendship

What do you consider the most important qualities in a friend? What makes a friend special? Think of the friends you really care about. What is it about them that you like? Write a well-organized, well-developed essay about this topic.

## Most Unforgettable Person

Who is the most unforgettable person you have ever met? What made that person unforgettable? Write an essay about that person.

## One Wish

If you could have only one wish, what would it be? In an essay, provide this information, and tell why you would choose this one wish.

## Environment

If you had the power to correct one environmental problem, what would you choose? Why would you choose this one? Write an essay on this topic.

## Reporter's Dream

If you were a newspaper reporter and you could cover any story, what story would you like to cover for the front page lead story? (E.g., it could be: "Cure for AIDS Found." "Man Makes First Contact With Extraterrestrial Civilization." etc.) Now write the story as if it were actually true.

### Difficult Choice

What is the most difficult decision you have ever had to make in your life? What factors did you consider in making your final decision? Write an essay on this topic.

### Worst Problem Facing Earth and Possible Solution

Write an essay about what you feel is the worst problem facing our planet, and give your suggested solution to this problem. Be sure to state the problem clearly and then to give your solution in an easy to follow and well organized paragraph or paragraphs. Include an introductory or topic sentence, body, and conclusion.

### Student Assessment of the Course

It is important to ask the students to share their assessment of this course with you. Ask them to write an essay and (1) to explain what this course involves; (2) to describe the learning environment; (3) to discuss the roles of the students and teacher in the office setting; (4) to talk about the course content, and finally (5) to give their opinions about the course. They should tell what they liked and what they didn't like about the course, and what they feel the course has done to help them improve their skills and how they feel about themselves.

Display some of their papers on the bulletin board, if possible, as these serve to inspire and motivate new students who are able to read what their peers have said about how the course helped them.

## CREATIVE WRITING

## Writing a Good Description

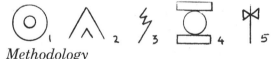

*Methodology*

1. Draw the doodles above on the chalkboard; give students small pieces of scratch paper and have them number from 1-5 and write what they see. For example, if they see a tire for #1, write tire; if they see a fried egg, write that.

2. After about 3-4 minutes, ask them what they saw for each doodle. Ask for 5 or 6 answers for each doodle, and be sure to get different interpretations of each doodle.

3. Now show them a color photograph (e.g., a magazine cover photo), and ask them to tell you what they see. This time their interpretations should be pretty much the same.

4. Next, ask them to try to analyze the difference between photos and doodles. What is it about the doodles that caused them all to look at the same one and see different things? What is it about the photograph that caused everyone to see the same thing in it? What does the photo have that the doodles lack? Have them answer until someone points out that the photo has more *details* than the doodles.

5. Go over definition of a description — A *description* is a word picture which you create from your impressions. Discuss why is it important to use specific words and details when writing your description. Also, discuss what we mean by "impressions," and, in particular, "sensory impressions."

6. Ask them why is it important to be able to write a good description? Which real life situations can they think of which would require that they be able to give a good description? Examples: witness to a crime; victim of a crime; lost pet; reporting a UFO sighting; job interview (self description); etc.

7. Go over a sample of a well-written description; pass out copies to them to look at as you read it.

8. Go over topics to select from and then give them the rest of the period to write a rough draft of one.

9. Monitor them as they write and look for introductory sentences, details, transition. etc. and a conclusion.

*Critical thinking skills used:*

**knowledge** of topic to write about

**comprehension** of instructions for assignment and of topic of essay.

**application** of material learned in lesson to the written essay. Also application of ability to write a good description to real life situations.

**analysis** of doodle and photograph and comparison of the two.

**synthesis** -production of an essay describing a situation.

*Topics for Descriptions (select one)*

1. You are the only eyewitness to a hit and run accident. Describe the accident. (Besides the written description, you may also draw a diagram showing how the accident occurred.)

2. Your pet is lost and you are posting a reward for anyone who finds it. Write a description of the lost pet.

3. You are the victim of an assault and robbery. Describe the person who assaulted and robbed you. Your description will be used by the police in order to find the suspect.

4. You are applying for a job which you really want to get. One requirement is that along with the application and resume, you submit a written one-page description of yourself. Include your strengths and weaknesses as well as personality traits, and any special or unique skills you have which make you qualified for the position.

5. You have witnessed a bank robbery. Describe the incident and the robbers in order to assist police in finding the guilty parties.

6. You have had a UFO sighting. Write a description of the object and include information about not only the object, but the atmospheric conditions, weather, trees, clouds, stars, etc. in front of or behind the object. Include such details as sound, shape, lighting, odors, and heat which were related to the object. Also include any effect the sighting appears to have had on humans, animals, the ground or trees, or automobile engines.

7. Write a description of a dental appointment during which you had a cavity filled. This is for someone who has never been to the dentist to read.

*Creative essays*

### If You Were A High School Principal

Write an essay on the following topic: If you were a high school principal, what would you do to make the students want to come to your school?

*Methodology*

*Prewriting*: Have them brainstorm suggestions and ideas for ways to motivate high school students to want to come to school. Afterward, ask them to analyze these and to discuss whether or not they are realistic and feasible. Now have them decide which ideas are related and could be grouped together, or which could be eliminated because they are repetitious of other ideas.

*Rough Draft*: Have them use their notes from the prewriting activities to write a rough draft of their essay. Editing: Have them now exchange their rough drafts with their partners and correct these or make suggestions for revisions and improvements.

*Revision*: Have them revise their rough drafts, inserting corrections, correcting spelling, using Writer's Helper to check grammar and then checking for capitalization, organization, punctuation, and spelling.

*Critical Thinking Skills Used*

**comprehension** of directions of the assignment.

**application** of knowledge of what motivates them or their fellow classmates to want to come to school, and applying that information to their plan as principal of the school.

**synthesis** of ideas into a finished written essay.

### Predicting the Future

Write an essay describing what our city (community) will be like in 100 years, in the year 2091. Include a discussion of the following subtopics:

**housing**: types of homes and availability of homes.

**transportation**: What type of transportation will there be? Will there be traffic congestion? Will there be public transportation?

**schools**: What will the schools be like? What types of schedules will there be for students during their typical school days?

What types of new subjects will students be studying then? Will the school buildings be different from those of the 1990s?

**recreation**: What will people in our city in 2091 do for recreation? Will golf and swimming still be popular? What sports will be popular? What other pastimes will be popular?

**environment**: What will our environment be like then? Will there be enough water to serve our residents? Where will the water come from? What will the air quality in our city be like in the year 2091? Will it be clean or will it be like L.A. and Phoenix are today?

**industry**: What types of industries will be located here in the year 2091?

## Methodology

Give them the topic for this week's essay, and as a prewriting exercise, discuss the subtopics above. Have them write them down and write down the questions for each one. Discuss the point that each subtopic should be a new paragraph, and that the questions listed for each subtopic should be answered in the paragraph about each respective subtopic. If they follow this formula, they should be starting new paragraphs at the correct points in their essay, and should have pertinent information furnished under each subtopic.

Have them brainstorm ideas for each one, especially those subtopics which require the most creative or imaginative thinking.

Next have them write the rough drafts and have their partners proofread and correct them before they edit and revise these to write the final drafts. They should also use all of the composition checklist tasks listed on their checklist pages.

## Critical thinking skills used

**knowledge** of current status of subtopics and of factors which will influence how they will change in the future.

**comprehension** of instructions and of topics being written about. Also, comprehension of how technology and other factors affect life at the time.

**application** of ideas brainstormed during prewriting activity to the actual writing of the essay. Also, application of the idea of organization of related topics into paragraphs.

**analysis** of how the technology and level of progress, as well as environmental factors in the year 2091 will affect the lifestyle of our city in that time.

**synthesis** of ideas discussed and brainstormed as well as thought of by the writer into a finished essay product.

**evaluation** of factors such as the environment in order to predict how they might affect our lifestyle in the year 2090.

*Cooperative Learning Lesson*
(duration: 2 weeks)
(Written report on what the high school of the future will be like)

*Implementation*

Students will work in heterogeneous groups to first list 10-15 learning outcomes that they feel high school graduates of the year 2000 should have. They will then rank order them in order of the highest to the lowest priority.

They will then write a group report in which they will describe their idea of the high school of the future which will equip its graduates with these learning outcomes. They will each write a portion of the report and will pass it in as one report with various sections. Also, as a group, they will make an oral presentation to the class on their respective sections of the report.

There will be distributed leadership as the students will assume the roles of:

• encourager/writer,

• reporter/writer,

• parliamentarian/writer.

Individual accountability will be accomplished because each student's section of the report will be graded on an individual basis.

Positive interdependence will be involved because if everyone in the group exhibits genuine effort and good writing skills in his/her section of the report, and if all sections of the report are passed in on time, and the oral presentations are judged by the teacher to be good quality, the group will earn 500 bonus points and will be excused from homework for a week.

## Instruction in Social Skills

The social skill of *seeking information and opinions* will be taught by means of a T-chart to show how it looks and sounds. This skill has been selected in order to ensure that all students participate actively, and that they each seek others' ideas and opinions. Students will be asked to practice doing and saying the things on the T-chart, and the teacher will observe each group and record this on small note pages which will then be given to each group.

Discuss the following aspects of your planned high school:

1. the building or physical plant itself
2. the courses to be taught at your school
3. any special or unique features in your school or any unique program you have (for example, your school might be underwater and teach about marine biology)
4. the schedule of courses for each day (will it be the same as that at the typical school today or will it be totally different?)
5. the location of your school and the population it serves (e.g., is it in the city, the country, the desert, the mountains, the seacoast, etc.?)

Students will be asked to talk among themselves and process how they accomplished getting the learning outcomes prioritized and how they managed to get everyone to write the report on time and so that all sections fit together in a logical and cohesive manner.

They will complete the statement : We reached consensus by _____and will be asked to share their answers with the class.

## SCHOOL OF THE FUTURE PROJECT

In this cooperative learning project, you will work in groups to plan a high school of the 21st century. Each person in the group will have an important role:

writers — 2 people who type reports on the computer

facilitator — makes sure everyone contributes ideas

timekeeper — makes sure everyone stays on task

reporters — everyone will be a reporter when it is time for the oral presentation for your group.

I. Make a list of 10 learning outcomes that you want graduates of your high school in the year 2000 to have. (These would include such things as: ability to get along with others, knowledge of academic subjects). These are the skills and knowledge that you feel are important for a person to succeed in the year 2000.

II. You are now going to design a high school of the future that will equip its graduates with the learning outcomes you just listed in part I. This will be a written report, and you will present an oral report on your school on _____. The written report will be passed in also. You must include the following things:

1. **Cover page** with title of your report and the names of people in your group. Also, include the date.

2. **Description** of the actual physical plant or school building. (Be creative. It doesn't have to be a 2-story brick building. It could be circular, or underwater (if it specializes in marine biology or oceanography), or in a solar-powered building, etc. It could be in a mall or office building, etc.

3. **Courses** to be taught at your school. Don't list every course. Simply explain what types of courses you will offer, and mention any particular emphasis your school may have, such as oceanography, job skills, etc.

4. **Schedule** of courses daily—Will it be the same as that of the typical school today, or will it be entirely different? If so, how?

5. Any **special or unique features** of your school? For example, a planetarium, or robotics lab.

6. Also tell **location** of your school and type of population you serve.

*Cooperative Learning Assignment*

## TELEVISION NEWSCAST FOR THE YEAR 2090

Imagine what sort of stories will make headlines in the news in 100 years in the year 2090. Write a newscast including the following segments:

• Cosmic News (of the whole universe)

• World and National News

• Local News

• Sports

• Weather Report

• Movie Review or Entertainment Report

Each person in your group must be an active participant in this newscast, both in writing segments of the news and in reading the news during your newscast.

You need to make up call letters for your station and a name for your newscast. It might be something as simple as Evening News, or you might be more imaginative.

You will receive a grade for the written and the oral portions of your report. You will be graded individually.

However, if your news team does a good job and everyone presents a well-thought out segment of the news (on time), your news team will earn 1500 bonus points. These may be used for various special events or privileges to be announced later.

Try to give some thought to the kinds of stories that might make the news in 100 years. Originality and creativity are important in this assignment. Also, the amount of effort evident by your newscast is going to make a difference in your grades.

You may use props and may add any additional features you like such as commercials, public service announcements, but make sure that these add to and do not take the place of the assigned segments of your newscast.

Your team will present its newscast on _____ date.

## PERSUASIVE WRITING

### Essay of Opinion

Read about an important issue facing the world at this time, and write an essay which first discusses this issue briefly, and secondly, gives your opinion on the issue and gives reasons for why you feel as you do.

## Methodology

Use the newspaper to give them some suggested topics: e.g., flag-burning, abortion, Star Wars Defense Initiative, AIDS legislation, funding for education in this country, or locally, capital punishment, civil rights, equality of the sexes, no pass- no play rule for students in Arizona, the expansion of our Space Program, teen pregnancy, teen suicide, the homeless, etc.

Give them a formula for organizing their essays:

I. Discuss specifically what the issue is that you are focussing on.

II. State how you stand on this issue.

III Give specific reasons why you feel as you do.

IV. Conclusion.

Have them proceed using the steps of the writing process, as in previous lessons, with a partner and with their composition checklist to use to indicate that they have followed the required procedure to edit and revise their papers and to finally write final drafts.

## Critical Thinking Skills Used

**knowledge** of the issue being discussed.

**comprehension** of the issue and of the assignment requirements.

**application** of the requirements of the assignment to the actual writing process.

**synthesis** by using the use of the information derived from the newspaper to produce an original written product.

**evaluation** of both sides of the issue in order to decide which stand to take.

## Essay of Persuasion

Write an essay for a particular person or population and try to convince them of something you feel strongly about. For example, try to convince your brother or sister to stop smoking, or to stop ditching classes. Other suggestions are:

- Convince your boss to give you a raise.
- Convince your parent to allow you to stay out later.
- Convince your friend not to drop out of school.
- Convince your Senator or Congressman to vote for a bill you support, or not to vote for a bill you don't support.
- Convince someone to hire you for the job of your dreams.
- Convince your father or mother to let you drive their car.
- Convince the bank loan officer to give you a loan to start a business of your own.

### *Methodology*

*Prewriting*: Discuss what makes a persuasive argument. Point out the need for strong, logical reasons to support your argument. Practice with them by giving them a topic to convince someone of and asking them to suggest reasons that might be convincing enough to persuade the person whom they are trying to convince.

*Drafting*: Have them write their arguments on the computers and then print out the rough drafts.

*Editing*: Have students exchange papers with partners who will read their arguments and tell them whether or not they feel they are convincing.

*Revising*: Have them insert corrections and changes into their essays and also follow the steps in their composition error checklists to be sure their papers are correctly written.

*Final Drafts*: Pass in final drafts with checklists attached.

### *Critical Thinking Skills Used*

**knowledge** of topic focussed on in essay.

**comprehension** of requirements of the assignment.

**application** of persuasive reasoning techniques to the written essay.

**synthesis** of ideas to produce written essay product.

**evaluation** of one another's papers to determine whether or not the arguments presented are effective and persuasive.

## Should Students Be Paid to Attend School?

Think carefully about the benefits and consequences of paying students to attend school. Jot some of these down on scratch paper and think about them. Then decide how you feel on this issue, and write a position paper in which you state if you are in favor or against this idea, and then offer specific reasons why you feel as you do.

## Seeing Both Sides of An Argument

Have them select a controversial topic, e.g., no pass, no play, and then have them write both sides of the argument so that they are able to see it from both sides. Finally, have them tell which view they hold, and then back it up with good reasons and evidence.

# 7

# Vocabulary Development

IN LINE WITH THE WHOLE LANGUAGE philosophy, several vehicles for building vocabulary skills are employed in this course. These are designed with the students and their interests in mind, as well as with the employment demands that will be placed on them in the future if they are to succeed in the workplace.

## VOCABULARY BUILDING SOFTWARE

The first of these vehicles for vocabulary instruction is computer software. As in the case of reading comprehension, computer programs can also be greatly effective in helping students to build vocabulary skills. They permit each student to move through the lessons at his or her own pace and to master the skills and material on an individualized basis. IBM's *Vocabulary Building Skills Software* is an effective package for teaching vocabulary. Students will progress through a series of lessons which include Greek and Latin prefixes and root words and include some very useful lists of vocabulary words. They will use the words in sentences as they progress, and they will also take quizzes and tests. (This program must be used with the Private Tutor disk.)

Davidson and Associates have produced a very appealing vocabulary package called *Word Attack* which includes word display, multiple choice (words and definitions), sentence completion using the vocabulary words, and a fast-paced fun game called Word Attack, which involves scoring points by matching synonyms and also shooting at moving targets for points. The program comes with a sheet for students to record their scores for each segment of each lesson.

Some programs include vocabulary instruction in the context of the stories or text used for reading comprehension improvement. For example, the *Reading Realities* series includes a Vocabulary Preview preceding each story. These include words and phrases or expressions which are included in the story, and which may not be familiar to the student. For example, the *Jury Series* includes many vocabulary terms relating to the criminal justice system in addition to other vocabulary words from the context of the various cases discussed.

The *Vocabulary Preview* gives students the word, the definition, a sentence containing the word, followed by synonyms of the word and an antonym for the word. Students will then come across the vocabulary word again in the process of reading the story.

Another program series which is excellent for vocabulary development is the *Carmen Sandiego* series of programs. These not only teach vocabulary words, they actually teach cultural literacy. In order to track down the criminals, students must know in which geographical location the criminal is located. The clues given include terms relating to foods, music, art, history, currency, and flags of the countries. Some examples of words that students might learn from working with these programs are: *lira, aria, drachmas, creole, ebony tresses, fugue, rubles, Rembrandt, spelunking.*

## GREEK AND LATIN PREFIXES AND ROOTS

Another helpful method of helping students to improve their vocabularies is to teach them Greek and Latin prefixes and root words and to have them then attempt to decode multisyllable words using these. For example, if a student knows that *circum* means "around," and *vene* means "go," then the student can deduce that *circumvent* means "to go around."

For students who speak foreign languages, especially Spanish, this is a particularly beneficial activity, since the root words are the same or very similar in so many languages. For example, if a student knows that in Spanish, "truth" is *verdad*, he or she can easily make the connection between the Spanish word and the English word *veracity*.

*Cooperative Learning*

## GREEK AND LATIN PREFIXES AND ROOT WORDS

*Implementation*

Students will work in heterogeneous groups to learn the meanings of 20 prefixes and root words (this will later be repeated for future lists) to ensure that everyone in the group learns the meanings of these.

*Roles:*

• encourager

• time keeper

• checker

Everyone signs a study sheet to signify that everyone in the group knows the prefixes and root words and their meanings. Individual accountability will be achieved through a test. If everyone in a group earns at least an 80% on the test, the group will earn 1000 bonus points. These may be used for the privilege of using fun software on Friday.

## Social Skill Acquisition

*Encouragement.* Show them what it looks like and sounds like with a T-chart. Also, review the social skill of checking for others' understanding of the work. Observe each group and give them a small piece of paper with feedback on their work social skills on it.

Have them **Process** and be able to tell us how they made sure that everyone in the group knew the list they were given to study. Did they have a system of memory devices? They will then be asked to share this with the class.

(practice noise signals)

Have them complete the sentence:

We did well on encouragement by_____and_____.

# PREFIXES AND ROOT WORDS STUDY SHEET

*ab* — go away
*ad* — to
*ami* — friend
*amore* — love
*ana* — against
*ante* — before
*anti* — against
*anthropo* — man
*astro* — star
*bellum* — war
*bene* — good
*bi* — two
*biblios* — book
*bio* — life
*capit* — head
*cardiac* — heart
*centi* — 100
*chrom* — color
*cian* — one who
*circum* — around
*cogn, scien* — to know
*corp* — body
*cosmos* — universe
*crac* — rule
*cred* — believe
*crypt* — secret
*de* — take away
*demo, popul* — people
*dermis* — skin
*dict* — speak, say
*dis* — out of
*dons, dentis* — tooth
*duc, duct* — to lead
*dyna* — power
*equ* — equal
*ex* — out, outside
*extra* — outside
*fac, fact* — make
*fid* — faithful
*flex* — bend

*frig,cryo* — cold
*graph* — writing
*here,hes* — stick
*hetero*-different
*homo* — same
*hydro* — water
*ideo* — idea
*inter* — between
*intra* — inside
*ject* — throw, hurl
*ject* — put in
*junct* — join
*juris* — justice
*latera* — side
*lect* — choose
*liber* — freedom
*log(y)* — study of
*magna* — great, large
*mal* — bad
*mand* — command
*mania* — madness
*manu* — hand
*meter* — measure
*micro* — tiny
*milli* — 1000
*mini* — small
*mitt,miss* — send
*mono* — one
*morph* — form
*multi* — many
*naut* — explorer
*nav* — ship
*nym* — name
*omni* — all, everywhere
*op* — eye
*orn* — bird
*ortho* — correct
*para* — alongside
*pater* — father
*path* — feeling

*patria* — country
*ped* — foot
*ped* — child
*pend* — hang, weigh
*penta,quin* — five
*peri* — around
*phagus* — eater
*phil* — love
*phobia* — fear
*phone* — sound
*phyte* — plant
*poly* — many
*pon* — put
*porta* — to carry
*post* — after
*pre* — before
*pseudo* — false
*quad, tetr* — four
*retro* — backward
*scrib* — write
*sent, sens* — feel
*sequ* — follow
*soph* — wisdom
*spect* — see, look
*sub* — under, below
*super* — greater
*syn* — together
*tact* — touch
*tech* — skill
*tele* — distant
*temp, chron* — time
*ten* — hold
*terra* — land, earth
*therm* — heat
*trans* — across
*tri* — three
*un, uni* — united
*ver* — truth
*vox* — voice
*zoo* — animal

## WORKSHEET

Use your knowledge of prefixes and root words to decode the meanings of these words:

subterranean _____

democracy _____

circumspect_____

postgraduate_____

trilingual _____

quadrilateral _____

minicomputer_____

astronaut_____

pericardium _____

antibiotic_____

beneficial_____

malfunction_____

predict _____

monochrome _____

telegraph_____

introspect _____

manuscript _____

intergalactic _____

credibility _____

periodontium _____

bibliography _____

## WORKSHEET

Can you decode the meanings of these words by using your prefixes and root words?

idiosyncracy _____

retroactive__,_____

quadrilateral _____

biped_____

pediatrics_____

malevolent _____

circumvent _____

introspect _____

veracity _____

cognizant_____

subterranean _____

triskadecaphobia_____

democracy_____

postbellum _____

anthropology_____

prerequisite _____

adhere _____

periodontium _____

amiable _____

benign _____

orthodontist _____

ornithology _____

## WORKSHEET

Try to decode these words by using your prefixes and root words to figure out their meanings.

retroactive_____

bilingual _____

polysyllabic_____

triskadecaphobia_____

prerequisite _____

sequential _____

millenium _____

precognition _____

cryptographer_____

amorous _____

ornithologist _____

malevolent _____

pseudopod _____

orthopedist _____

omnipotent _____

morphological_____

cognizant_____

retrospect _____

contradict _____

antedate_____

circumspect_____

intervene _____

## COINING YOUR OWN WORDS

One method of making the study of Greek and Latin prefixes and root words interesting to students is to allow them to be creative and to use these prefixes and root words to invent their own words. They are to also write definitions for their word coinages.

Prior to giving them this assignment, model for them how this may be done. Some examples are the following:

*minisubhydromobile* — small underwater vehicle

*minisubterraquadriped* — small underground four-footed animal

*magnadentiphobia* — great fear of dentists

*triburger* — triple burger

Also, point out how many words have had to be invented to name new inventions or new technological developments. Some examples are: zipper, lunar landing module (LEM), radar, space shuttle, microwave oven, cryogenics, videodisc player.

### *Bulletin Board Display:*

A neat idea for a bulletin board display is to take the best of the students' coinages and to write them on large coins made of colored construction paper and place them on the bulletin board.

## VOCABULARY FROM LITERATURE

Literature is also a natural tool from which to teach new vocabulary words. Encourage students to try to figure out the meanings of the words from context clues, as well as from the prefixes or root words they have learned. Also, the newspaper is another fertile area for vocabulary growth. One strategy to apply here is to have each group of three students locate in the newspaper each day three words whose meaning they do not know. They may do this as a cooperative learning exercise and then have them look up the words in the dictionary, use them in sentences, and teach them to one another until they have mastered them well enough that they are able to teach them to the rest of the class at an office meeting.

## SUMMARY

It is vital to emphasize to the students that words are more powerful than weapons and that an excellent vocabulary attributes power to an individual. It is important for them to understand the value of a good working vocabulary.

# 8

# Career Research and Exploration

ONE OF THE MOST EFFECTIVE links to success is the setting of goals for performance. Goals play a significant role in developing self-motivation and self-direction for students. Goals are personal standards by which students may assess their performances (Alderman, 28).

Short-term goals which are specific in regard to the criterion for success in a particular assignment are generally the most effective with at-risk students. For this reason, most of the software programs for these students as well as the reading comprehension learning strategy discussed earlier all have progress charts on which students may record and plot their progress.

However, as the students in this English course approach graduation from high school, this is an appropriate and opportune time to focus on long-term goals and on the importance of looking ahead, and planning for the future. It has been my experience that it is not sufficient to set high school graduation as your goal for your at-risk students. In the highly technological age of the '90s, most jobs in the employment arena will require post-high school training. *Even if your students make great strides in self-esteem and in attitude, they will need your encouragement and guidance to plan beyond high school graduation.*

One of the best ways to accomplish this is to invite several people in the community to serve as guest speakers about their respective careers. Try to expose your students to as wide a range of careers as possible. Poll the students to determine some of the careers in which they are interested. Often students are not aware of many careers other than those paying minimum wage because of the socioeconomic environment in which they live. Also, many of these students do not see themselves in a career other than a minimum wage job, so they close their eyes to any other possibility. Thus, do not limit the guest speakers to those careers suggested by students.

In addition, require them to research a career of their choice. A career research project is outlined on the succeeding page. This is especially important for all juniors and seniors.

If at all possible, try to arrange for employers to conduct mock job interviews, and have your students submit business letters, resumes, and applications for hypothetical positions of their choice. Also, try to make arrangements for the students who do the best job on the letter, resume, application and interview to spend a day shadowing persons in those careers.

The community is a fertile resource ground for this type of thing, and that, if approached properly, most employers are not only willing, but are also enthusiastic about participating in such a program.

The *Reading Realities* "Career Preparation" software is an excellent vehicle for providing students with an opportunity to do some career exploration. Careers covered include: computer programmer, secretary, actress, sportscaster, doctor, banker, lawyer, photographer, inventor, owner of small business, teacher, pilot, hairdresser, interior designer, and chef. The teacher's looseleaf binder which comes with the program also contains several creative as well as practical activities as follow-up assignments.

Looking ahead and setting long-range goals also serve to boost students' self-esteem. After all, one must be a worthwhile person in order to have career goals and positive future plans.

Also, if students are able to see a transfer between their classwork and the real employment world, they are more likely to become self-motivated and self-directed learners who will work to their fullest potential in class. Learning takes place more effectively if students understand why they are learning the particular material being covered in class and how it applies to them in a practical sense. Career preparation and job skills are two areas which students will perceive as indeed having direct benefits and practical application for them in their lives.

*(Student handout)*

## CAREER RESEARCH PROJECT

It is important to have goals and to plan ahead in order to prepare for the career of your choice. Some people have an idea what they'd like to do after high school, but have no idea whatsoever what they need to do to prepare for that career. Most jobs now will require some training beyond high school, so it is a good idea to do some research into what the educational requirements are for the career you select.

You are to do some research and find out the following information to pass in for a report by _____.

What preparation or training do you need for this career?

Is this type of training available in our community or would you have to travel elsewhere to get it?

What are the job possibilities in this career in our state? If you were in a different part of the U.S. with this career, what would the job possibilities be like?

What is an average day in the life of a person in this career like?

What is the average pay for a person in this career?

Are there any health restrictions or requirements for this career?

You may obtain this information in a variety of ways. One of the best ways is to interview someone already holding this job. You may check with the library. You may write to businesses involved in this career and ask them for information, which they will send you.

## JOB SKILLS

In addition to career research, career shadowing, and mock job interviews, teach them how to write a business letter with the correct format as well as how to write a proper resume, and how to complete employment applications. Employers are frequently quite willing to give teachers copies of job applications so that future prospective job applicants will be better prepared. Have students practice on several of these applications and critique them very carefully. Stress to them that it is far better to have a teacher throw out your application than to have an employer do so. Learning to correctly fill out applications for employment can make a significant difference in one's future job experience.

*Cooperative Learning Lesson*

## WRITE A CORRECT BUSINESS LETTER

*Implementation*

Students will work in small heterogeneous groups to learn the correct format of a business letter, and to actually write business letters as cover letters for inclusion with job applications for a hypothetical job. They will proofread one another's papers to ensure that they all adhere to the proper format of a business letter and that they are clearly written and error-free. Everyone in the group must sign on the model letter provided for the group in order to signify that they can each write a correct business letter with the proper format without having a model to copy.

This will be part of a unit on job applications, resumes, business letters, and mock job interviews. Students will be individually graded on their business letters. If everyone in the group earns at least a B on the letter, that group will be given an opportunity to do career shadowing if the teacher is able to arrange it.

The group roles will be as follows:

facilitator/editor
encourager/editor
timekeeper/editor

*Process*

They will be asked to process how they learned the correct format for a business letter and will be able to remember it. They will also be asked to explain how they will be able to apply this skill in real life. The social skill of checking for others' understanding of the work will be taught because it will be important to have everyone know how to write a correct business letter without having to look at a model. A T-chart will be used to teach this.

They will be asked to complete the sentence: In any group it is helpful to _____ and _____. They will be asked to share their answers and to explain how they can apply this skill in real life.

## COVER LETTER TO APPLY FOR A JOB

State that your resume is *enclosed*.

If you are answering an ad, explain *where* and *when* you saw it, and *what job* was advertised.

If there was no ad and you are sending the resume on your own, tell *what type of job* you are looking for.

Explain *why you are interested* in the job, *why you feel you are qualified* for it. You need not give lots of details about yourself, however, since that is what the resume is for.

At the end of the letter *ask for an interview* and give a *phone number* where you can be reached.

A cover letter should be *brief and to the point*. Keep it simple. Be sure to check spelling, grammar, punctuation, and use the correct format and margins, and spacing.

# 9

# Parental Involvement

INVOLVING PARENTS IN THE EDUCATION of their children is crucial in helping students to experience success in school and to develop self-esteem. Parents, as the first teachers children come into contact with, have a powerful influence in molding their children's attitudes toward learning.

One of the best methods for involving parents and for helping them to develop their own self-esteem is to initiate an adult literacy program one or two evenings per week. This may be accomplished through a partnership between your program and a local community college or through the adult basic education program in your community. The course will be held in your classroom lab, and you will teach it, but it will be funded through one of the sources suggested in the preceding sentence.

Ask for students to volunteer to assist the parents in the evening classes. Since adults tend to be more intimidated by computers than do teens, (especially if they have never used computers before), it will be very helpful to have students there to assist with the adult class.

Once you establish an adult class for parents, you will have a *family literacy program*. This is an extremely effective vehicle for helping your students to feel more positive about themselves, about their families, and about education. In addition, parents will develop their own self-esteem, and will improve their employability as they improve their literacy and job skills. Consequently, they will be capable of helping their children to develop and nurture their own self-esteem.

You will find adults delightful to teach. In the beginning, they are likely to be quite anxious and quite intimidated by the idea of being back in school. The classroom setting as a professional office environment helps to lower their level of anxiety and also serves to eradicate the stigma of a literacy class. This will cause them to be more comfortable with the idea of going to class. Sometimes they will even refer to it as a computer class.

As time goes on and they become comfortable in the class, they will participate more actively. Adults are extremely excited about learning and very appreciative of efforts to help them. Learning how to use the computers is very satisfying for them, and it is delightful to observe them developing self-confidence and taking great pride in learning how to use high tech equipment. Give them as much encouragement as possible. They will need it, and they will respond positively to it.

In addition to the computer programs discussed in this volume in the chapters on reading comprehension, writing skills, and vocabulary development, there are other components which should be incorporated into the curriculum for the adult class.

As a part of the curriculum for the class, use the list of Greek and Latin prefixes and root words in the chapter on Vocabulary Development in this volume, and employ them in this cooperative learning activity geared for adults.

Each week go over ten prefixes and root words and their meanings with the class as a group. Have them give examples of words which have these prefixes and root words. Then have them work in pairs to teach one another these ten prefixes and root words and their meanings. As soon as they are certain that both people in their pair can give the correct meanings of at least eight of the ten prefixes and root words they studied, they are to raise their hands to indicate that they are ready to be quizzed. Give each member of the pair an oral quiz on the meanings of the ten prefixes and root words. If they are both able to answer at least eight of them correctly, give them 100 bonus points.

Have them work with the same partners throughout the course, and repeat the procedure each week for the next ten prefixes and root words until they learn the entire list.

Then at the Awards Evening at the culmination of the course, those pairs earning the highest amount of bonus points for vocabulary development will be given gift certificates for dinners at local restaurants.

This is a particularly appealing concept for adults, as the restaurant gift certificates serve to motivate them without the pressure of grades threatening them. Also, one of the best ways to learn something is to teach it to someone else, so this activity effectively reinforces their learning of these prefixes and root words.

Several weeks prior to the Awards Evening, send several letters to local restaurants explaining about the program and telling about this particular learning activity with prefixes and root words. Ask them to contribute gift certificates to be used to motivate these students to excel. In my experience, restaurant owners are more than happy to contribute to this activity, and many of them have sent gift certificates to be used for this purpose.

Another aspect of the program which I have found to work extremely effectively with adults is the RAP strategy. This is the paraphrasing strategy (to improve reading comprehension) which is discussed in the chapter on reading comprehension. Teach it to them and then have them use it during the first 10 or 15 minutes of the class every week. Several adults have told me that they have used this learning strategy to read and comprehend their textbooks for other courses they are taking at the community college or in adult basic education classes and that they have found it really helps them. One student, in particular, stressed how much the RAP strategy helped her in comprehending the reading material in her textbook for her course on social work.

Another beneficial component to include in the curriculum for the class is a unit on job skills. Obtain sample employment applications from several businesses and have them practice filling them out. You will find that many of the adult students do not know how to complete an employment application or do not follow directions in completing it. For example, they may write in sections of the applications which are clearly marked to be completed by employer only.

Teach them to write a personal resume also and have them save these on their disks in addition to printing them. Tell them that as long as they are in the class, they can update their resumes and submit them with employment applications for actual jobs.

During this unit also teach them to write a correct business letter with the proper format. Have them practice by writing a cover letter for a hypothetical job, and attaching a resume and application form with it.

Finally, arrange for a guest speaker who will address the topic of job interviews and how to act and dress during a job interview. This is a particularly beneficial experience for adult classes I have taught. Speakers generally offer many practical points as to how to do an effective job of selling or promoting oneself to a prospective employer during an interview.

At the conclusion of the semester, plan an awards evening for this class. Make it a special event, and ask everyone to bring some refreshments. Ask the parents to invite their children and anyone else they would like to have present at the ceremony. Present the students with certificates and awards.

In Arizona, the Secretary of State will provide beautiful engraved certificates for all graduates of literacy programs. These are parchment and have the seal of the state on them. Adults especially enjoy receiving them, and I generally ask a dignitary such as the Chief Justice of the Arizona Supreme Court to present them. This all contributes toward the realization for the students that completion of this course is an important step in improving their lives and their futures. It is very possible that other states offer the same or similar certificates. Contact your Secretary of State's office to inquire about this.

Also, during the course, employ some cooperative learning activities such as the prefixes and root words activity described in chapter seven. Then, at the awards ceremony possibly present gift certificates to those groups which earned the highest amount of bonus points during the cooperative learning activities. I have received a great deal of gift certificates from the business sector as a result of simply sending letters about the family literacy program to area businesses to ask for donations of gift certificate to be used as awards for cooperative learning activities. The response has been overwhelming, and at the adults awards ceremony, every student receives a gift certificate for dinner for two, often from a fine restaurant.

This is mentioned again only to reiterate that the community is generally extremely supportive of literacy programs, and, in particular, of those which include two generations of family. It is important to involve as many community resources as partners for your program as possible. This not only enhances and enriches your students' learning experiences, it also serves to inform and educate the public and the business sector about the good things that are occurring in our public schools and the need for funding of such programs.

Another highlight of the adult awards evening is to have father and daughter speeches or mother and son speeches. It will probably be necessary for you to assist them with writing the speeches and then to practice with them for several evenings prior to the awards evening. In my experience, these speeches have been one of the most exciting events in the program and have resulted in the parents and children becoming closer and in building mutual respect for one another.

Yet another feature of the adult awards ceremony has been to include a musical performance by one of the students. In one of our awards ceremonies, one student sang lively Mexican songs and accompanied himself on the guitar. This added a festive atmosphere to the evening and kept the students and guests on a very upbeat note.

The adult class is probably the most fun to teach. An added bonus of this class is that there are funds available through grants for financing family literacy programs now. Contact your state department of education for possible information. Also, inquire about federal grants for such programs.

Another important resource for family literacy programs which is sponsored by ASCD (Association for Supervision and Curriculum Development) is a professional network to increase awareness of the issues and to facilitate communication among existing family literacy programs. Anyone interested in organizing a family or intergenerational literacy program in conjunction with your program for at-risk students, may obtain further information on this network by contacting Maryann E. Nuckolls, Facilitator of ASCD's Intergenerational/Family Literacy Network, 1336 W. Knox, Tucson, AZ 85705, (602) 292-9676. The network will put you in touch with programs and persons who can assist you in this endeavor (Nuckolls, 45).

As with the high school students, it is important to give your adult students as many opportunities as possible to experience success. Many of them have not had this type of opportunity for years and view themselves as failures who have no possibility of ever changing their situations in life. Increasing their own self-esteem will enable them to help their children to also develop their self-esteem and self-confidence as well.

The experience of returning to school will generally not only cause them to value education more, but will also cause them to become closer to their children, who are high school students.

One of the parents in my adult class who was a speaker at the Awards Evening for his class summed it up very eloquently when he said, "This is our second chance to be somebody in life, and we all want to succeed this time, and I'm sure we will. We just need time and nice people to help us out and we will be all set. I'd like to close my speech with this statement, 'Someday I'd like to be just like my daughter.'"

# 10

# Public Relations

## COMBATTING THE STIGMA OF A LITERACY PROGRAM

IN ORDER TO COMBAT THE POSSIBLE STIGMA of a "literacy" program, it is important to have a good public relations program. Publicize your students' successes. Whenever possible, take advantage of any opportunity to get good press or good public relations. Other students need to know that this classroom is a "cool" or "ok" place, and that it is not a room for dummies. It helps to stress the idea of the use of high tech computer equipment to teach students how to improve reading and writing skills. When you have some good news from the program, notify the school newspaper or the school newsletter for parents. Sometimes it is possible to allow a student competing in a statewide contest for something such as writing computer graphics programs to use the computers after school. My students have typed the programs for school events and once made personalized stationery for all of the teachers and administrators on Teacher Appreciation Day. This gets the message out that good things are happening in this class, and that it is a place where you learn skills you can employ in the real job world.

It is not easy to build this image, but it is important that you do so. Your students need to feel that their classroom is not a place they need to feel ashamed to attend. It should be a place they feel privileged and excited to attend.

Also, be sure to have your students write their impressions of the program and be certain to keep copies of these. These are great for posting on bulletin boards and for having new students read in order to get an idea of what the program is like. It will also furnish you with some helpful insights into how students feel about the program. In addition, you will want to use these students' views of the program as part of your documentation of the success of the program. It is useful to include some of these papers in any annual or semi-annual reports you generate for your program or for any publications you produce for your program.

## ESTABLISH PARTNERSHIPS WITH BUSINESSES AND ORGANIZATIONS

Your program will be much more enriched and your students will be that much better served if you are able to establish partnerships with businesses or organizations in the community. Through these partnerships, your students may have opportunities to participate in mock job interviews, career shadowing, field trips, or scholarships for college. Area businesses are more than willing to donate gift certificates to be used to motivate students to do well in school. You may use these as awards for various types of achievement or for contest prizes.

## WRIGHT FLIGHT

One of the most exciting organizations with whom I have established a partnership is called Wright Flight. This is a non-profit organization named after Orville and Wilbur Wright, which helps kids to reach new heights in academic achievement and in self-esteem. The organization is largely made up of civilian and Air Force pilots who work with at-risk students and get students to establish academic goals for themselves and to build self-esteem. When they achieve their goals, and learn about the history of flight and the principles of aviation, they are able to earn free flying lessons from Wright Flight. The flight experience is free of charge to the student. After the flying lesson, the student receives a commemorative T-shirt and certificate. Often a photographer is present to take the student's photograph with the pilot and the aircraft. Wright Flight is currently serving approximately 65 Tucson schools and has provided thousands of free flying lessons to students from middle school to high school ages.

Civic and community organizations such as Kiwanis sponsor fly days three or four times per year. These are the days that hundreds of students and their teachers meet at the airport for refreshments and flying lessons. Fly days are generally on Saturdays. Parents and friends may watch as the students take off with their instructor pilots for their flying lessons. The program has been highly motivational for countless teenagers and has done wonders to improve thousands of students' attitudes.

The Wright Flight organization was founded by Capt. Robin Stoddard, and the organization now has chapters in other states, and is planning to become national, with chapters in fifty states. For information on organizing a Wright Flight chapter in your state, contact:

Wright Flight
1300 E. Valencia #300
Tucson, AZ 85706
Tel: (602) 294-0404

In addition to Wright Flight or other civic organizations, try to establish partnerships with as many businesses as you can. For instance, invite five or six companies to enter into partnerships with you to teach students about a variety of careers. Ask them to send guest speakers to acquaint your students with a wide range of careers they might be interested in entering. Then have the students send cover letters, employment applications, and resumes to apply for jobs that sound appealing to them. Actually send the letters to the companies and ask them to select the best ones for each career and then to conduct mock job interviews with those students. Finally, ask them to invite the students to spend a day career shadowing with persons in the jobs they applied for. This has been an area which has worked extremely well for our program, and I have found businesses more than happy to participate. One point which generally wins over the employers is to simply remind them that today's students are tomorrow's workforce, so that their investment in these students will eventually benefit the companies.

## PRINT A BROCHURE ABOUT YOUR PROGRAM

If possible print a brochure with information about your course, and include in it some students' comments about your program. If your course is highly effective, you can anticipate many inquiries for information about it from parents, educators, the media, etc., and it is helpful to have printed information readily available to distribute to them.

## BE A 24-HOUR PUBLIC RELATIONS PERSON

In a decade when the general public is so down on public education, it is imperative that every public school employee, particularly teachers, all work as public relations persons for education on a 24-hour basis. When in the supermarket, share the good news about the accomplishments of your students and your program with others. Any taxpayer is an important client of public education, and if the clients are satisfied with the job the schools are doing, it will translate into increased funding for education at election time. Cold though it may seem, this is the harsh reality of the 90s.

Be sure to keep informed as to who your district administrators are and who your school board members are. Make it a point to invite them to visit your classroom and familiarize themselves with your program. The average term of Superintendents of Schools and Assistant Superintendents of Schools in a district today is less than five years. Therefore, it is important to invite each new Superintendent of Schools or Assistant Superintendent of Schools to visit the program.

## MAINTAIN A DATABASE TO DOCUMENT STUDENT PERFORMANCE

It is important to maintain a complete database of student data and to keep it updated. Some of the information that should be recorded includes such items as:

- Student's name (Also assign an ID number to each student)
- Age
- Grade level (9, 10, 11, or 12)
- Sex
- Ethnic background
- Reading pretest scores
- Reading post-test scores
- Early and later writing samples (scored holistically)
- Any other information which is necessary or helpful to your particular program.

Use a database program which will enable you to print out lists, totals, or averages according to whatever information fields you designate.

It is imperative to be able to document student improvement. In order to obtain continued funding for your course, you must be able to show quantitatively that students are, in fact, making significant growth in reading and writing skills. You may also wish to obtain narrative data from other teachers, parents, or employers of the students to document their growth of self-esteem and improvement of attitude.

Remember that you will be the person who will have to sell the program to the administration. The more documentation you can accumulate to illustrate the success and effectiveness of the program, the easier your job will be, and the more support you will receive from the community and the administration.

## PROMOTE YOUR DISTRICT — NOT SIMPLY YOUR PROGRAM

As an educator and district employee, it is important to promote the district, not simply your particular program. Although it is not correct logic and is certainly not fair, the public tends to generalize about education district-wide on the basis of any negative perceptions they have about just about anything in the entire district. For example, a woman visited me from a civic organization which was considering making a donation to a college scholarship fund for our students who graduate from high school. Although she felt that our program is extremely worthwhile, she complained to me that an acquaintance of hers told her that the staff members in the district administration office take too many coffee breaks and waste taxpayers' money. Consequently, our students could have lost potential scholarship funds because of a taxpayer's perception, accurate or inaccurate, of others in the district, who have no relationship to our program.

Unfortunately, this situation is not unique. Indeed, how many times have we judged a restaurant by the cleanliness of its restrooms? How often have we expressed a lack of confidence in an airline if the seats are faded or the carpet on the floor is stained? How confident have we been in an airline if our luggage has not arrived at our destination on time?

If our respective programs can lose public support because of any number of things which might jaundice the public's perception of education in the district, then conversely, if the public perceives anything negative about our particular program, that could jaundice the public perception of the entire district as well.

The bottom line is that perceptions, whether correct or not, can either contribute greatly or detract tremendously from your program. There is no question that the extra effort we educators put forth to be full-time public relations persons will be a worthwhile investment.

# Bibliography

Advanced computer system improves adult reading and writing skills. (1987). *Optical information systems*, May–June, 140–141.

Alderman, Kay (1990). Motivation for at-risk students. *Educational Leadership*,September, 27–30.

*Arizona supreme court PALS resource book*. (1988).

Barbour, Andrew. (1989). Meeting the literacy challenge. *Electronic Learning*,January-February, 4–8.

Bernardon, Nancy Lynn. (1989, January). Let's erase illiteracy from the workplace. *Personnel*, January, 29–32.

Bruder, Isabelle. (1989, Jan-Feb). Overcoming the dropout problem. *Electronic Learning*, January-February, 16–17.

Christensen, Marge (1990). *An assessment of the principle of the alphabet literacy system (PALS) program at an inner city high school in Tucson and its effects on four diverse target populations*. (Master's Degree thesis).

Dishon, Dee and O'Leary, Pat Wilson. (1984). *A guidebook for cooperative learning: A technique for creating more effective schools*. Holmes Beach, FL: Learning Publications.

Dunseith school dedicates IBM computer lab. (1988). *Turtle Mountain Star*, North Dakota, July 25.

Ellison, Carol (1989). PC's in the schools—An American tragedy. *PC Computing*, January, 97–104.

Gordon, Gayle (1989). Arizona's involvement with PALS. *The Learning Post*, May, 10–11.

Gursky, Daniel (1991). After the reign of Dick and Jane. *Teacher Magazine*. August, 22–27.

A hot connection: Criminal justice and literacy (1989). *The Learning Post*, May, 10.

How can businesses fight workplace illiteracy? (1989). *Training and Development Journal*, January, 18–25.

An innovative funding scheme has schools going dutch in Kentucky. (1989). *Electronic Learning*, January-February.

International Business Machines (IBM) (1989a). *Evaluations of IBM literacy programs*.

IBM. (1987b) *InfoCourse: Principle of the alphabet literacy system planning and implementation guide*.

IBM. (1988c) *News about InfoWindow in corrections rehabilitation*.

IBM. (1988d) *Principle of the alphabet literacy system*.

IBM. (May, 1989e) *Writing to read and principle of the alphabet literacy system outcomes: The latest, May, 1989*.

Investing in America's future. (1989). *Electronic Learning*, January-February, 9–11.

Karlstein, Patricia (1988). Fighting high school illiteracy: The PALS project in Brooklyn. *T.H.E. Journal.* Special Issue, 49–54.

Lavin, Richard J. and Jean E. Sanders (1988). Using computers as tools for reducing adult literacy. *T.H.E. Journal,* June, 68–70.

Leinfuss, Emily (1986). IBM joins war on illiteracy. *MIS Week.* November 3, 62.

Loftis, Lorraine (1989). Introducing Kenosha, Wisconsin. *Pen Pals,* July, 9.

Martin, John Henry. (1986a). *IBM InfoCourse: Principle of the alphabet literacy system.* Atlanta: IBM Corp, Advanced Education Systems.

Martin, John Henry. (1983b). *A Report of a field test of the principle of the alphabet literacy system.* Florida: JHM Corporation.

McBroom, Tammy (1987). Unique program offers students chance to learn our language. *Kansas City Kansan,* November 8.

Miller, Charles (1989). IBM InfoWindow—A new kind of peripheral. *Optical Information Systems,* May-June, 217–218.

Nasella, Susan (1988), Firms fight worker illiteracy. *Tampa Bay Business,* April 24–30, 5–6.

Neder, Barbara (1989). Joint efforts. *The Learning Post,* May, 7.

Nuckolls, Maryann E. (1991). Expanding students' potential through family literacy. *Educational Leadership,* September, 45.

*Passing the word.* (1988). Illinois Literacy Council, October-November.

Phillips, Nancye M. (1989, January). A Life of Lessons. *PC Computing.* pp. 106–112.

Ralph, John. (1989, Jan). Improving Education for the Disadvantaged: Do We Know Whom to Help? *Phi Delta Kappan.* pp. 395–401.

Robertson, Judith. (1989a). *An Assessment of a High School PALS Lab, Tucson, AZ.* (U.S. Dept. of Education: Educational Research Grant).

Robertson, Judith. (1989b, May). Partnerships Work. *The Learning Post.* p. 6.

Roscow, La Vergne. (1988, Nov). Adult Illiterates Offer Unexpected Cues into the Reading Process. *Journal of Reading.* 38 (2). pp. 120–124.

Staley, Pat. (1987, November 25). To Read—to Understand. *Penasee Globe.* Michigan. pp. 8–9.

Starting All Over Again. (1989, Jan-Feb), *Electronic Learning.* pp. 18–19.

Technology and the At-Risk Student. (1988, Nov-Dec). *Electronic Learning.* pp.35–49.

Texas Center for Adult Literacy and Learning of the Adult & Extension Education Program, College of Education, Texas A & M University (undated). *An Evaluation of Computer-Assisted Instructional Systems Used to Deliver Literacy Services for J.T.P.A. Participants at Houston Community College.*

*Toward a State of Self-Esteem* (The Final Report of the California Task Force to Promote Self-Esteem and Personal and Social Responsibility). (1990, Jan.). California State Dept. of Education.

Turner, Terrilyn. (1988, June). An Overview of Computers in Adult Literacy Programs. *Lifelong Learning.* 11 (8). pp. 9–12.

*Unlocking the Future: Adult Literacy in Arizona.* (1986, December). (Report of the Governor and Superintendent's Joint Task Force on Adult Literacy).

# DO YOU HAVE AN IDEA TO SHARE?

The National Educational Service is always looking for high-quality manuscripts that have practical applications for educators and others who work with youth.

Do you have a new, innovative, or especially effective approach to some timely issue? Does one of your colleagues have something burning to say on curriculum development, professionalism in education, excellence in teaching, or some other aspect of education? If so, let us know. We would like to hear from you. Tell us that reading Marge Christensen's book gave you an incentive to contact us.

Nancy Shin, Director of Publications
National Educational Service
1610 West Third Street
P.O. Box 8
Bloomington, IN  47402
(800) 733-6786
(812) 336-7700

*Motivational English for At-Risk Students: A Language Arts Course that Works* is one of the many publications produced by the National Educational Service. Our mission is to provide you and other leaders in education, business, and government with timely, top-quality publications, videos, and conferences. If you have any questions or comments about *Motivational English for At-Risk Students: A Language Arts Course that Works* or if you want information on in-service training or professional development on any of the following topics:

Discipline with Dignity
Reclaiming Youth at Risk
Cooperative Learning
Thinking Across the Curriculum
Cooperative Management
Parental Involvement

Contact us at:

**National Educational Service**
**1610 West Third Street**
**P.O. Box 8**
**Bloomington, IN 47402**
**(812) 336-7700**
**(800)733-6786**

**(812) 336-7790 (FAX)**

# NEED MORE COPIES?

Need more copies of this book? Want your own copy? If so, you can order additional copies of *Motivational English for At-Risk Students: A Language Arts Course That Works*, using this form or by calling (812) 336-7700 or (800) 733-6786 (US only). You can send the orders by FAX at (812) 336-7790.

We guarantee complete satisfaction with all of our materials. If you are not completely satisfied with any NES publication, you can return it to us within 30 days for a full refund.

|  | Quantity | Total Price |
|---|---|---|
| *Motivational English for At-Risk Students:* *A Language Arts Course that Works* ($16.95 each) | _____ | _____ |

Quantity discounts:    10–19 copies—save 10%
                          20–45 copies—save 20%
                          46–99 copies—save 35%
                          100 + copies—save 50%

Shipping: Add $1.50 per copy
(There is no shipping charge when you *include* payment with your order)        _____
Indiana Residents add 5% sales tax        _____

                                TOTAL    _____

☐   Check enclosed with order      ☐   Please bill me
                                      P.O.# _____
☐   Money Order                     ☐   VISA or MasterCard
                                      Account # _____
                                      Exp. Date_____

Cardholder Signature _____

Ship to:

Name _____ Title _____

Organization _____

Address _____

City _____

State _____ZIP _____

Phone # _____

## MAIL TO:
## National Educational Service
## 1610 West Third Street
## P.O. Box 8
## Bloomington, IN 47402